WYDANIE NARODOWE
DZIEŁ FRYDERYKA CHOPINA

NATIONAL EDITION
OF THE WORKS OF FRYDERYK CHOPIN

CONCERTO in E minor Op. 11

FOR PIANO AND ORCHESTRA

version for one piano

NATIONAL EDITION
Edited by JAN EKIER

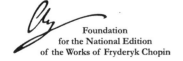

Foundation
for the National Edition
of the Works of Fryderyk Chopin

PWM
EDITION

SERIES A. WORKS PUBLISHED DURING CHOPIN'S LIFETIME. VOLUME XIIIa

FRYDERYK CHOPIN

KONCERT e-moll op. 11
NA FORTEPIAN I ORKIESTRĘ
wersja na jeden fortepian

WYDANIE NARODOWE
Redaktor naczelny: JAN EKIER

FUNDACJA WYDANIA NARODOWEGO
POLSKIE WYDAWNICTWO MUZYCZNE SA
WARSZAWA 2022

SERIA A. UTWORY WYDANE ZA ŻYCIA CHOPINA. TOM XIIIa

Redakcja tomu: Jan Ekier, Paweł Kamiński

Komentarz wykonawczy i Komentarz źródłowy (skrócony) dołączone są do nut głównej
serii *Wydania Narodowego* oraz do strony internetowej www.chopin-nationaledition.com

Pełne *Komentarze źródłowe* do poszczególnych tomów wydawane są oddzielnie.

Wydany w oddzielnym tomie *Wstęp do Wydania Narodowego Dzieł Fryderyka Chopina
– 1. Zagadnienia edytorskie* obejmuje całokształt ogólnych problemów wydawniczych,
zaś *Wstęp… – 2. Zagadnienia wykonawcze* – całokształt ogólnych problemów interpretacyjnych.
Pierwsza część *Wstępu* jest także dostępna na stronie www.pwm.com.pl

Partytura *Koncertu* w wersji historycznej, zestawiona z głosów pierwszego wydania, tworzy tom 18 **A XVb**,
partytura w wersji koncertowej, odtworzona przy uwzględnieniu także innych źródeł
przekazujących intencję Chopina, tworzy tom 33 **B VIIIa**.
Wersja z drugim fortepianem, zawierającym wyciąg partii orkiestry, tworzy tom 30 **B VIa**.

Editors of this Volume: Jan Ekier, Paweł Kamiński

A *Performance Commentary* and a *Source Commentary (abridged)* are included in the
music of the main series of the *National Edition* and available on www.chopin-nationaledition.com

Full *Source Commentaries* on each volume are published separately.

The *Introduction to the National Edition of the Works of Fryderyk Chopin
1. Editorial Problems*, published as a separate volume, covers general matters concerning the publication.
The *Introduction… 2. Problems of Performance* covers all general questions of the interpretation.
First part of the *Introduction* is also available on the website www.pwm.com.pl

The historical version of the score of the *Concerto,* composed of parts from the first edition, forms volume 18 **A XVb**,
and the concert version of the score, recreated by taking into consideration
also other sources which present Chopin's intention, constitutes volume 33 **B VIIIa**.
The version with the second piano, containing the reduction of the orchestra part, forms volume 30 **B VIa**.

Koncert e-moll op. 11 / Concerto in E minor Op. 11

o Koncercie e-moll ...

„Ernemann był u mnie, osądził, że I-sze Allegro lepsze w nowym Koncercie – [...] nagli robota; trzeba pisać na gwałt."

17 kwietnia

„Rondo do nowego Koncertu nie skończone – a do tego trzeba weny; nawet się z nim nie spieszę, bo mając pierwsze Allegro, o resztę się nie troszczę. [...] Adagio od nowego Koncertu jest E-dur. Nie ma to być mocne, jest ono więcej romansowe, spokojne, melancholiczne, powinno czynić wrażenie miłego spojrzenia w miejsce, gdzie stawa tysiąc lubych przypomnień na myśli. – Jest to jakieś dumanie w piękny czas wiosnowy, ale przy księżycu. Dlatego też akompaniuję go s o r d i n a m i, to jest skrzypcami przytłumionymi gatunkiem grzebieni, które okraczając strony dają im jakiś nosowy, srebrny tonik. – Może to jest złe, ale czemu się wstydzić źle pisać pomimo swojej wiedzy – skutek dopiero błąd okaże."

15 maja

„[...] już w tym tygodniu mam cały Koncert próbować w kwartecie, dlatego żeby najprzód ten kwartet mógł się porozumieć ze mną – trocha oswoić, bez czego, Elsner powiada, próba z orkiestrą od razu nie przyszłaby do ładu. Linowski przepisuje na gwałt, ale już Rondo zaczął."

31 sierpnia

„Próbowałem zeszłej środy mój Koncert w kwartecie. Kontent byłem, ale nie bardzo – mówią ludzie, że ostatni finał najładniejszy (bo najzrozumialszy). Jak się wyda z orkiestrą, napiszę Ci w przyszły tydzień, bo w tę środę spróbuję."

18 września

„[...] dziś próbuję drugi Koncert z kompletną orkiestrą prócz trąb i kotłów, [...] Ja już drugi Koncert skończyłem, a jeszcze taki hebes [głupi], jak przed zaczęciem poznawania klawiszy. [...] muszę lecieć jeszcze się zapewnić o Elsnerze, [...] pulpitach i s o r d i n a c h, o których wczoraj na śmierć zapomniałem; bez nich bowiem Adagio by upadło, którego powodzenie i tak wielkie być nie może, ile mi się zdaje. Rondo e f e k t o w n e, Allegro m o c n e. O, przeklęta miłości własna!"

22 września

„Po próbie orkiestrowej 2-go Koncertu stanęła decyzja, żeby go publicznie grać, i w przyszły poniedziałek, to jest 11-go tego miesiąca, wystąpię z nim. Jak z jednej strony nierad jestem temu, tak z drugiej ciekaw jestem ogólnego efektu. Rondo, myślę, że na wszystkich zrobi wrażenie. Na to bowiem Rondo Soliwa mi powiedział: «il vous fait beaucoup d'honneur» [przynosi panu duży zaszczyt], Kurpiński o oryginalności, Elsner o rytmie prawił."

5 października

„Wczorajszy koncert udał mi się – pospieszam z tym doniesieniem. Powiadam Aśpanu, żem się wcale a wcale nie bał, grał tak, jak kiedy sam jestem, i dobrze było. Pełna sala. Goernera Symfonia zaczęła. Potem moja mość Allegro e-moll, które, jak z płatka wywinął, na Streycherowskim fortepianie się wydać miało. Brawa huczne. Soliwa kontent; dyrygował z powodu swojej arii z chórem, którą Panna Wołkow, ubrana jak aniołek w niebieskim, ładnie odśpiewała; po tej arii Adagio i Rondo nastąpiło, po którym pauza między 1-szą a drugą częścią. – [...] Gdyby był Soliwa nie wziął moich partycji do domu, nie przejrzał i nie dyrygował tak, że nie mogłem lecieć na złamanie karku, nie wiem, jakby wczoraj było, ale tak nas umiał zawsze wszystkich utrzymać, że nigdy, powiadam Ci, jeszcze z orkiestrą tak mi się spokojnie grać nie zdarzyło. Fortepian bardzo się miał podobać a Panna Wołkow jeszcze bardziej."

12 października

Z listów F. Chopina do Tytusa Woyciechowskiego w Poturzynie, Warszawa 1830.

„Znajdowaliśmy się właśnie w tutejszej resursie, gdzie Schnabel, kapellmeister, prosił, ażebym był obecny
na próbie z mającego się dać wieczorem koncertu. [...] Schnabel, co mię od czterech lat nie słyszał, prosił,
ażebym spróbował fortepian. Trudno było odmówić, siadłem i zagrałem parę wariacji. [...] zaczęli mię prosić,
ażebym wieczorem dał się słyszeć. Szczególniej Schnabel tak szczerze nalegał, że nie śmiałem staremu odmówić. [...]
Pojechałem tedy z jego synem po nuty i zagrałem im Romans i Rondo z II Koncertu. Na próbie
dziwili się Niemcy mojej grze: «Was für ein leichtes Spiel hat er» [Jakie on ma lekkie uderzenie], mówili,
a o kompozycji nic. [...] Ponieważ ja jeszcze nie mam ustalonej reputacji, więc dziwiono się i bano dziwić;
nie wiedzieli, czy kompozycja dobra, czy też im się tak tylko stale wydaje. Jeden z tutejszych znawców
przybliżył się do mnie i chwalił nowość formy, mówiąc, że mu się nic jeszcze w tej formie nie zdarzyło słyszeć,
nie wiem, kto to był ale ten mię może najlepiej zrozumiał."

F. Chopin do Rodziny w Warszawie, Wrocław 9 XI 1830.

„Chopin miał szczęśliwy pomysł wykonania adagia [Romance. Larghetto] ze swego ostatniego koncertu.
Umieszczona pomiędzy dwoma utworami orkiestrowymi o gwałtownym stylu, owa zachwycająca kompozycja,
której nieodparty urok idzie w parze z najgłębszą myślą religijną, pogrążyła słuchaczy w swoistej radości –
spokojnej i ekstatycznej, do której nie przywykliśmy w podobnej sytuacji. Wszystko to różni się bardzo
od ciągnących się w nieskończoność adagiów, które wypełniają zazwyczaj środek koncertu fortepianowego;
jest tu tyle prostoty połączonej z taką świeżością wyobraźni, że gdy ostatnia nuta spadła niby perła do złotej wazy,
publiczność pogrążona w kontemplacji powstrzymała się przez kilka chwil od oklasków, słuchała nadal.
Tak właśnie, śledząc harmonijne opadanie półcieni wieczornego zmierzchu, pozostajemy bez ruchu
w ciemności z oczami utkwionymi ciągle w ten punkt horyzontu, gdzie właśnie zniknęło światło."

Hector Berlioz „Le Rénovateur" 3 (IV), 5 I 1835.

„Pianista powinien tutaj stać się pierwszym tenorem, pierwszym sopranem, zawsze śpiewakiem
i to brawurowym we wszystkich pasażach, które – zgodnie z wolą Chopina – należało koniecznie
oddać w stylu cantabile. Takie rozumienie pierwszej części wpajał swojemu ulubieńcowi, Filtschowi.
Sam Chopin nie wykonywał już wówczas (1842) tego utworu, gdyż zrezygnował z występów publicznych.
Grał nam jednak tematy – w sposób nieopisanie piękny, a także szkicował pasaże. Chciał aby grać je cantabile,
z pewnym umiarem głośności i brawury, poprzez uwydatnienie każdej cząstki motywicznej i nadzwyczaj delikatne
uderzenie, nawet w przejściowych pasażach, co jest tu wyjątkiem. Nie było nigdy mowy o drugiej i trzeciej części. [...]
Filtsch studiował pierwszą część, opracowując każde solo oddzielnie; Chopin nigdy nie pozwalał mu
wykonać tej części od początku do końca, gdyż bardzo się nią wzruszał. Uważał też, że każde solo
zawiera w sobie całość utworu. Kiedy w końcu pozwolił Filtschowi wykonać całość [...],
Mistrz rzekł: «Opracowałeś już tę część tak pięknie, że możemy ją wykonać: ja będę twoją orkiestrą».
[W salonie Chopina, dla specjalnie zaproszonego grona osób, którego większość stanowiły
uczennice z wyższej arystokracji, wykonali na dwa fortepiany pierwszą część Koncertu e-moll].
Chopin w swym niezrównanym akompaniamencie odtworzył całą przemyślaną, zwiewną instrumentację
tego utworu. Grał z pamięci. Nigdy nie słyszałem czegoś, co dałoby się porównać z pierwszym tutti,
oddanym przez niego na fortepianie. Mały czynił cuda. Wszystko razem pozostawiało wrażenie na całe życie."

Wilhelm von Lenz, Uebersichtliche Beurtheilung der Pianoforte-Kompositionen von Chopin [...], „Neue Berliner Musikzeitung" 4 IX 1872.

about the Concerto in E minor ...

"Ernemann paid me a visit and judged that the first Allegro is better in the new Concerto – [...] the task is urgent; I have to write in a hurry."

17 April

"The Rondo for the new Concerto is not completed – and to do this I need inspiration; I am not in a particular hurry since having completed the first Allegro and am not anxious about the rest. [...] The Adagio to the new Concerto is in E major. It is not supposed to be emphatic, but more in a sentimental vein, tranquil and melancholic, and should produce the impression of gazing at a spot which brings to mind a thousand pleasant memories. – It resembles beautiful springtime reflections, albeit by moonlight. This is the reason why I accompany it by means of s o r d i n i, in other words, violins muffled with kind of combs which, by bestriding the strings, produce a nasal, silver tone. – This might be wrong, but why should one be ashamed of writing faultily despite knowledge – only the outcome will disclose the error."

15 May

"[...] I am to rehearse the whole Concerto with a quartet already this week, so that the quartet could first become acquainted with me – to grow somewhat familiar, without which, Elsner claims, a rehearsal with an orchestra would not succeed. Linowski is copying hurriedly, but he has already started the Rondo."

31 August

"Last Wednesday I rehearsed my Concerto with a quartet. I was content but not very much so – people say that the last finale was the most pleasant (since it was the most comprehensible). I shall write you next week how it will sound with an orchestra because I shall rehearse it this Wednesday."

18 September

"[...] today I am rehearsing the second Concerto with the whole orchestra, with the exception of trumpets and kettledrums, [...] I have already completed the second Concerto, but am still as foolish as I was before I learned the keyboard. [...] I must fly to once again assure myself about Elsner, [...] the music stands and s o r d i n i, about which I totally forgot yesterday; without them the Adagio, whose success, I suppose, does not seem to be great anyhow, would fail. The Rondo is e f f e c t i v e, the Allegro is f o r c e f u l. O, cursed self-love!"

22 September

"After an orchestra rehearsal of the second Concerto it was decided to perform it in public; I shall present it next Monday, that is, on the eleventh of the month. On the one hand, I am not very pleased with this, but, on the other hand, I am curious about the general effect. I believe that the Rondo will make an impression on everyone. It is about this Rondo that Soliva told me: 'il vous fait beaucoup d'honneur' [it does great credit to you], Kurpiński mentioned originality, and Elsner spoke about rhythm."

5 October

"I hasten to tell you that yesterday's concert was a success. I inform your Lordship that I was not at all nervous, and played as I do when I am alone, and that everything went well. Full hall. First, Görner's symphony, followed by my lordship, the Allegro in E minor, which I reeled off with ease, was presented on a Streicher piano. Tumultuous applause. Soliva was delighted; he conducted because of his air with chorus, beautifully sung by Mlle Wołkow dressed prettily like a cherub in blue; after the air came the Adagio and the Rondo; then a pause between the first and second parts. – [...] I really do not know how things would have gone yesterday if Soliva had not taken my scores home, read them and conducted so that I did not have play rapidly as though to break my neck, but he managed so well to hold us back that, I assure you, I have never succeeded in playing so comfortably with an orchestra. The piano, it seems, was much liked, and Mlle Wołkow even more so."

12 October

From the letters of F. Chopin to Tytus Woyciechowski in Poturzyn, Warsaw 1830.

*"We found ourselves at the Resource where kappelmeister Schnabel requested that I be present at the rehearsal
of a concert to be performed in the evening. [...] Schnabel, who has not heard me for four years,
asked me to try the piano. It was difficult to refuse, so I sat down and played several variations.
[...] they started to ask me to play in the evening. Schnabel in particular insisted so earnestly that I did not dare
to refuse the old man. [...] I went, therefore, with his son to get the music and played to them the Romance
and the Rondo from the second Concerto. During the rehearsal, the Germans were astonished by my performance:
'Was für ein leichtes Spiel hat er' [What a light touch he has], but said nothing about the composition. [...]
Since I still do not have an established reputation they were surprised and, simultaneously, afraid to be surprised;
they did not know whether the composition is good or whether it only appeared to be so.
One of the local connoisseurs approached me and praised the novelty of form, saying that
he had never heard anything similar; I do not know who he was, but he probably understood me best of all."*

F. Chopin to his family in Warsaw, Wrocław 9 November 1830.

*"Chopin had the fortunate idea of playing the Adagio [Romance. Larghetto] from his last Concerto.
Placed between two orchestral compositions maintained in a turbulent style, this enchanting work,
in which irresistible charm is combined with most profound religious thoughts, submerged the listeners
into a specific joy – serene and ecstatic – to which we have not become accustomed in a similar situation.
All this differs greatly from the endless adagios, which usually fill the middle movement of a piano concerto;
in this case, there is so much simplicity used with such freshness of imagination, that when the last note was heard,
in the manner of a pearl cast into a golden vase, the audience, immersed in contemplation, continued to listen,
and for a few moments restrained itself from applauding. In the same way, while observing the harmonious descent
of twilight semi-shadows, we remain motionless in the darkness, with our eyes still focused on that point of the horizon,
where the light has just faded."*

Hector Berlioz "Le Rénovateur" 3 (IV), 5 January 1835.

*"The pianist should become here the first tenor and the first soprano, but, predominantly, a singer
and an excellent one in all those arpeggios which – in accordance with Chopin's will – should be performed
in the cantabile style. This is the way he taught his beloved Filtsch to understand this movement.
At the time (1842) Chopin no longer performed the composition, since he had resigned from public appearances.
Nonetheless, he played to us the themes in an indescribably beautiful way and outlined the passages.
He wanted them to be executed cantabile, with a certain moderation of loudness and bravura,
by emphasizing each motif particle and with extraordinarily delicate sounding even in the transitory passages,
which here is regarded as an exception. No mention was ever made about the second and third movement.
[...] Filtsch studied the first movement working on each solo separately; Chopin had never permitted him
to perform this movement from the beginning to the end, because he became excessively stirred.
He was also of the opinion that each solo contained the whole composition.
When he finally allowed Filtsch to play the whole work [...], the Master declared:
'You have prepared this movement so splendidly that we can perform it: I shall be your orchestra'.
[In the Chopin salon, they performed the first movement of the Concerto in E minor on two pianos
for a specially invited audience, whose majority was composed of pupils from aristocratic families].
Chopin recreated the whole well-devised, ephemeral instrumentation of this composition in his incomparable
accompaniment. He played by heart. Never before have I heard anything to equal the first tutti, performed by him
on the piano. The boy worked miracles. The overall effect produced an impression to last a lifetime."*

Wilhelm von Lenz, *Uebersichtliche Beurtheilung der Pianoforte-Kompositionen von Chopin [...]*, "Neue Berliner Musikzeitung" 4 September 1872.

Concerto pour le piano avec accompagnement d'orchestre

A Monsieur F. Kalkbrenner

op. 11

* Trudne do odczytania palcowanie wpisane przez Chopina do egzemplarza lekcyjnego - patrz *Komentarz wykonawczy*.
  The fingering, difficult to decipher, added by Chopin in a pupil's copy - *vide Performance Commentary*.

* Patrz *Komentarz wykonawczy.*
  Vide Performance Commentary.

* W źródłach *ritenuto* umieszczone jest - prawdopodobnie błędnie - już pod koniec t. 281. Patrz *Komentarz źródłowy.*
  In the sources *ritenuto* is placed, probably mistakenly, already at the end of bar 281. *Vide Source Commentary.*

23

24

30

* Inne palcowanie - patrz *Komentarz wykonawczy*.
For different fingering *vide Performance Commentary*.

31

* Zdaniem redakcji górne dźwięki - *e¹* w t. 463, *fis* w t. 464 i *h* w t. 465 - należy powtarzać.
  In the editors' opinion, the upper notes - *e¹* in bar 463, *f#* in bar 464 and *b* in bar 465 - should be repeated.

34

* W źródłach prawdopodobnie błędnie:
  The sources have, probably mistakenly:

35

* Patrz *Komentarz wykonawczy* do t. 185 i 540.
  Vide Performance Commentary to bars 185 and 540.

* Patrz *Komentarz wykonawczy* do t. 227-229.
Vide Performance Commentary to bars 227-229.

** Wersja pierwszych wydań, być może błędna:
The version in the original editions, possibly erroneous:

Patrz *Komentarz źródłowy i wykonawczy.*
Vide Source and *Performance Commentaries.*

*** Dopuszczalny wariant:
Admissible variant:

Patrz *Komentarz źródłowy.*
Vide Source Commentary.

* Patrz *Komentarz wykonawczy.*
Vide Performance Commentary.

** Wersja źródłowa, przypuszczalnie błędna: . Patrz *Komentarz źródłowy.*
Source version, possibly erroneous: . *Vide Source Commentary.*

39

* Patrz *Komentarz wykonawczy.*
  Vide Performance Commentary.

** Wykonanie jak w t. 329-332.
   Execution as in bars 329-332.

FWN 13 **A XIIIa**

ROMANCE

* Patrz *Komentarz wykonawczy.*
  Vide Performance Commentary.

* Wersja pierwszych wydań, prawdopodobnie błędna: . Patrz *Komentarz źródłowy*.
Version in the original editions, probably mistaken: . *Vide Source Commentary*.

* Patrz *Komentarz wykonawczy.*
  Vide Performance Commentary.

** Patrz *Komentarz źródłowy.*
   Vide Source Commentary.

*** Wpisany do egzemplarza lekcyjnego pasaż zamiast w t. 59 można wykonać w t. 61:   . Patrz *Komentarz źródłowy* i *wykonawczy.*
     The arpeggio recorded in a pupil's copy can be performed in bar 61 instead of bar 59:   . *Vide Source* and *Performance Commentaries.*

* Wariant rytmiczny ostatniej ćwierćnuty taktu: ♩♩♩♩ . Można go zastosować do każdej z podanych wersji melodii. Patrz *Komentarz źródłowy*.
The rhythmic variant of the last beat: ♩♩♩♩ . It can be applied in each of the given versions of the melody. *Vide Source Commentary*.

FWN 13 **A XIIIa**

* Propozycja pedalizacji - patrz *Komentarz wykonawczy*.
For a proposal of pedalling *vide Performance Commentary*.

49

50

RONDO

* Wersje podstawy basowej nale y uzgodnić z orkiestrą (drugim fortepianem). Patrz *Komentarz źródłowy* i *wykonawczy*.
  Versions of the bass note should be coordinated with the orchestra (second piano). *Vide Source* and *Performance Commentaries*.

64

66

* Patrz *Komentarz wykonawczy.*
  Vide *Performance Commentary.*

Okładka i opracowanie graficzne · Cover design and graphics: MARIA EKIER
Tłumaczenie angielskie · English translation: ALEKSANDRA RODZIŃSKA-CHOJNOWSKA

Fundacja Wydania Narodowego Dzieł Fryderyka Chopina
ul. Okólnik 2, pok. 405, 00-368 Warszawa
www.chopin-nationaledition.com

Polskie Wydawnictwo Muzyczne SA
al. Krasińskiego 11a, 31-111 Kraków
www.pwm.com.pl

Wyd. I. Printed in Poland 2022. Drukarnia REGIS Sp. z o.o.
ul. Napoleona 4, 05-230 Kobyłka

ISBN 83-89003-60-0

NATIONAL EDITION OF THE WORKS OF FRYDERYK CHOPIN

Plan of the edition

Series A. WORKS PUBLISHED DURING CHOPIN'S LIFETIME

1	**A I**	**Ballades** Opp. 23, 38, 47, 52
2	**A II**	**Etudes** Opp. 10, 25, Three Etudes (Méthode des Méthodes)
3	**A III**	**Impromptus** Opp. 29, 36, 51
4	**A IV**	**Mazurkas (A)** Opp. 6, 7, 17, 24, 30, 33, 41, Mazurka in a (Gaillard), Mazurka in a (from the album La France Musicale /Notre Temps/), Opp. 50, 56, 59, 63
5	**A V**	**Nocturnes** Opp. 9, 15, 27, 32, 37, 48, 55, 62
6	**A VI**	**Polonaises (A)** Opp. 26, 40, 44, 53, 61
7	**A VII**	**Preludes** Opp. 28, 45
8	**A VIII**	**Rondos** Opp. 1, 5, 16
9	**A IX**	**Scherzos** Opp. 20, 31, 39, 54
10	**A X**	**Sonatas** Opp. 35, 58
11	**A XI**	**Waltzes (A)** Opp. 18, 34, 42, 64
12	**A XII**	**Various Works (A)** Variations brillantes Op. 12, Bolero, Tarantella, Allegro de concert, Fantaisie Op. 49, Berceuse, Barcarolle; *supplement* – Variation VI from "Hexameron"
13	**A XIIIa**	**Concerto in E minor** Op. 11 for piano and orchestra (version for one piano)
14	**A XIIIb**	**Concerto in F minor** Op. 21 for piano and orchestra (version for one piano)
15	**A XIVa**	**Concert Works** for piano and orchestra Opp. 2, 13, 14 (version for one piano)
16	**A XIVb**	**Grande Polonaise in E♭ major** Op. 22 for piano and orchestra (version for one piano)
17	**A XVa**	**Variations on "Là ci darem" from "Don Giovanni"** Op. 2. Score
18	**A XVb**	**Concerto in E minor** Op. 11. Score (historical version)
19	**A XVc**	**Fantasia on Polish Airs** Op. 13. Score
20	**A XVd**	**Krakowiak** Op. 14. Score
21	**A XVe**	**Concerto in F minor** Op. 21. Score (historical version)
22	**A XVf**	**Grande Polonaise in E♭ major** Op. 22. Score
23	**A XVI**	**Works for Piano and Cello** Polonaise Op. 3, Grand Duo Concertant, Sonata Op. 65
24	**A XVII**	**Piano Trio** Op. 8

Series B. WORKS PUBLISHED POSTHUMOUSLY

(The titles in square brackets [] have been reconstructed by the National Edition; the titles in slant marks // are still in use today but are definitely, or very probably, not authentic)

25	**B I**	**Mazurkas (B)** in B♭, G, a, C, F, G, B♭, A♭, C, a, g, f
26	**B II**	**Polonaises (B)** in B♭, g, A♭, g♯, d, f, b♭, B♭, G♭
27	**B III**	**Waltzes (B)** in E, b, D♭, A♭, e, G♭, A♭, f, a
28	**B IV**	**Various Works (B)** Variations in E, Sonata in c (Op. 4)
29	**B V**	**Various Compositions** Funeral March in c, [Variants] /Souvenir de Paganini/, Nocturne in e, Ecossaises in D, G, D♭, Contredanse, [Allegretto], Lento con gran espressione /Nocturne in c♯/, Cantabile in B♭, Presto con leggierezza /Prelude in A♭/, Impromptu in c♯ /Fantaisie-Impromptu/, "Spring" (version for piano), Sostenuto /Waltz in E♭/, Moderato /Feuille d'Album/, Galop Marquis, Nocturne in c
30	**B VIa**	**Concerto in E minor** Op. 11 for piano and orchestra (version with second piano)
31	**B VIb**	**Concerto in F minor** Op. 21 for piano and orchestra (version with second piano)
32	**B VII**	**Concert Works** for piano and orchestra Opp. 2, 13, 14, 22 (version with second piano)
33	**B VIIIa**	**Concerto in E minor** Op. 11. Score (concert version)
34	**B VIIIb**	**Concerto in F minor** Op. 21. Score (concert version)
35	**B IX**	**Rondo in C** for two pianos; **Variations in D** for four hands; *addendum* – working version of Rondo in C (for one piano)
36	**B X**	**Songs**

| 37 | **Supplement** Compositions partly by Chopin: Hexameron, Mazurkas in F♯, D, D, C, Variations for Flute and Piano; harmonizations of songs and dances: "The Dąbrowski Mazurka", "God who hast embraced Poland" (Largo) Bourrées in G, A, Allegretto in A-major/minor |

WYDANIE NARODOWE DZIEŁ FRYDERYKA CHOPINA

Plan edycji

Seria A. UTWORY WYDANE ZA ŻYCIA CHOPINA

Seria B. UTWORY WYDANE POŚMIERTNIE

(Tytuły w nawiasach kwadratowych [] są tytułami zrekonstruowanymi przez WN, tytuły w nawiasach prostych // są dotychczas używanymi, z pewnością lub dużym prawdopodobieństwem, nieautentycznymi tytułami)

1 **A I**   **Ballady** op. 23, 38, 47, 52

2 **A II**   **Etiudy** op. 10, 25, Trzy Etiudy (Méthode des Méthodes)

3 **A III**   **Impromptus** op. 29, 36, 51

4 **A IV**   **Mazurki (A)** op. 6, 7, 17, 24, 30, 33, 41, Mazurek a (Gaillard), Mazurek a (z albumu La France Musicale /Notre Temps/), op. 50, 56, 59, 63

25 **B I**   **Mazurki (B)** B, G, a, C, F, G, B, As, C, a, g, f

5 **A V**   **Nokturny** op. 9, 15, 27, 32, 37, 48, 55, 62

6 **A VI**   **Polonezy (A)** op. 26, 40, 44, 53, 61

26 **B II**   **Polonezy (B)** B, g, As, gis, d, f, b, B, Ges

7 **A VII**   **Preludia** op. 28, 45

8 **A VIII**   **Ronda** op. 1, 5, 16

9 **A IX**   **Scherza** op. 20, 31, 39, 54

10 **A X**   **Sonaty** op. 35, 58

11 **A XI**   **Walce (A)** op. 18, 34, 42, 64

27 **B III**   **Walce (B)** E, h, Des, As, e, Ges, As, f, a

12 **A XII**   **Dzieła różne (A)** Variations brillantes op. 12, Bolero, Tarantela, Allegro de concert, Fantazja op. 49, Berceuse, Barkarola; *suplement* – Wariacja VI z „Hexameronu"

28 **B IV**   **Dzieła różne (B)** Wariacje E, Sonata c (op. 4)

29 **B V**   **Różne utwory** Marsz żałobny c, [Warianty] /Souvenir de Paganini/, Nokturn e, Ecossaises D, G, Des, Kontredans, [Allegretto], Lento con gran espressione /Nokturn cis/, Cantabile B, Presto con leggierezza /Preludium As/, Impromptu cis /Fantaisie-Impromptu/, „Wiosna" (wersja na fortepian), Sostenuto /Walc Es/, Moderato /Kartka z albumu/, Galop Marquis, Nokturn c

13 **A XIIIa**   **Koncert e-moll** op. 11 na fortepian i orkiestrę (wersja na jeden fortepian)

30 **B VIa**   **Koncert e-moll** op. 11 na fortepian i orkiestrę (wersja z drugim fortepianem)

14 **A XIIIb**   **Koncert f-moll** op. 21 na fortepian i orkiestrę (wersja na jeden fortepian)

31 **B VIb**   **Koncert f-moll** op. 21 na fortepian i orkiestrę (wersja z drugim fortepianem)

15 **A XIVa**   **Utwory koncertowe** na fortepian i orkiestrę op. 2, 13, 14 (wersja na jeden fortepian)

32 **B VII**   **Utwory koncertowe** na fortepian i orkiestrę op. 2, 13, 14, 22 (wersja z drugim fortepianem)

16 **A XIVb**   **Polonez Es-dur** op. 22 na fortepian i orkiestrę (wersja na jeden fortepian)

17 **A XVa**   **Wariacje na temat z *Don Giovanniego* Mozarta** op. 2. Partytura

18 **A XVb**   **Koncert e-moll** op. 11. Partytura (wersja historyczna)

33 **B VIIIa**   **Koncert e-moll** op. 11. Partytura (wersja koncertowa)

19 **A XVc**   **Fantazja na tematy polskie** op. 13. Partytura

20 **A XVd**   **Krakowiak** op. 14. Partytura

21 **A XVe**   **Koncert f-moll** op. 21. Partytura (wersja historyczna)

34 **B VIIIb**   **Koncert f-moll** op. 21. Partytura (wersja koncertowa)

22 **A XVf**   **Polonez Es-dur** op. 22. Partytura

23 **A XVI**   **Utwory na fortepian i wiolonczelę** Polonez op. 3, Grand Duo Concertant, Sonata op. 65

35 **B IX**   **Rondo C-dur** na dwa fortepiany; **Wariacje D-dur** na 4 ręce; *dodatek* – wersja robocza Ronda C-dur (na jeden fortepian)

24 **A XVII**   **Trio na fortepian, skrzypce i wiolonczelę** op. 8

36 **B X**   **Pieśni i piosnki**

37 **Suplement** Utwory częściowego autorstwa Chopina: Hexameron, Mazurki Fis, D, D, C, Wariacje na flet i fortepian; harmonizacje pieśni i tańców: „Mazurek Dąbrowskiego", „Boże, coś Polskę" (Largo), Bourrées G, A, Allegretto A-dur/a-moll

FRYDERYK CHOPIN
CONCERTO in E minor Op. 11
version for one piano

Performance Commentary
Source Commentary (abridged)

PERFORMANCE COMMENTARY

Introductory remarks

During Chopin's lifetime his *Piano Concertos* were performed in four versions:
1. The version for one piano. This editorial form, fundamental at the time, of compositions for the piano with an orchestra accompaniment – solo piano in normal print, *tutti* and certain soli of orchestral instruments in smaller print – was also a form of presenting the work in salons and even in concert halls, as evidenced by author's variants applied "in execution without accompaniment", occurring in Chopin's smaller concert works (op. 2, 14) and a handwritten annotation made by the composer in a pupil's copy of the *Concerto in F minor* op. 21, containing also this type of a variant (a left hand harmonic accompaniment to the recitative in the second movement, bars 45-72). We cannot exclude the possibility that Chopin himself performed in public the version for one piano of the *Concerto in E minor*.
Orchestral parts supplemented the printed form of this version. It was possible to purchase a complete set for full orchestra or quintet parts only.
2. The version with a second piano was used while playing at home, during lessons (cf. quotations *about the Concerto...*, prior to the musical text, the statement by W. von Lenz), and sometimes at public concerts. However, piano reductions of the orchestra part in Chopin's *Concertos* were not published until about 1860. Earlier, use was made of handwritten reductions (extant reductions of the second and third movement of both *Concertos* were made by Chopin's friends J. Fontana and A. Franchomme). Owing to the fact that the *Concerto* was not published in this version during the composer's lifetime, the *National Edition* presents it in series B.
3. The version with a string quartet (quintet) was used both during concerts and in salons. In 1829, Chopin wrote to T. Woyciechowski: "Every Friday Kessler holds small musical meetings [...] A fortnight ago, there was Ries' *Concerto* in a quartet" (see also quotations *About the Concerto...*, prior to the musical text, letters from 31 August and 18 September 1830). This version was played from the parts of the string instruments, which included the more important soli of the wind instruments.
4. The composer intended the version with the orchestra to be the basic one. Upon several occasions, Chopin himself played in public this version of the *Concerto in E minor*. The score made up of the original orchestral parts from the Parisian original edition of the *Concerto* was never published. The first score, issued by Kistner in approximately 1865, already contained slight changes.

Notes on the musical text

The variants marked as *ossia* were given this label by Chopin or were added in his hand to pupils' copies; variants without this designation are the result of discrepancies in the texts of authentic versions or an inability to establish an unambiguous reading of the text.
Minor authentic alternatives (single notes, ornaments, slurs, accents, pedal indications, etc.) that can be regarded as variants are enclosed in round brackets ( ), whilst editorial additions are written in square brackets [ ].
Pianists who are not interested in editorial questions, and want to base their performance on a single text, unhampered by variants, are recommended to use the music printed in the principal staves, including all the markings in brackets.
Chopin's original fingering is indicated in large bold-type numerals, **1 2 3 4 5**, in contrast to the editors' fingering which is written in small italic numerals, *1 2 3 4 5*. Wherever authentic fingering is enclosed in parentheses this means that it was not present in the primary sources, but added by Chopin to his pupils' copies. The dashed signs indicating the distribution of parts between the hands come from the editors.
A general discussion on the interpretation of Chopin's works is to be contained in a separate volume: *The Introduction to the National Edition*, in the section entitled *Problems of Performance*.

Abbreviations: R.H. – right hand, L.H. – left hand

Concerto in E minor, op. 11

Attention should be drawn to the proper realisation of the authentic slurring. Short slurs, characteristic for this period in Chopin's oeuvre, usually do not encompass whole phrases – the beginnings of the slurs should be accentuated by delicate pressure, but the player should be warned against lifting the hand when the end of a slur occurs within a phrase.
In general, the realisation of individual grace-notes does not pose a problem: in the majority of cases, it is unessential whether the grace-note is executed in an anticipatory manner or – in accordance with classical rules – on the downbeat; it is only important that it be played as quickly as possible and with distinct articulation. Situations in which one of the above possibilities appears to be clearly closer to Chopin's style are discussed below in commentaries to particular bars.

I. Allegro maestoso

p. 16   *Bar 140 and 148-149* The notation of the arpeggios in the form of separate wavy lines for each hand does not determine the manner of their realisation. They can be executed in a continuous way (1) or simultaneously in both hands (2). The editors recommend arpeggiation only in L.H. (3), which grants the chords a more decisive nature without losing the impression of an arpeggio.

Bar 141 In the opinion of the editors, the moment of depressing the pedal can be shifted a crotchet later in order to avoid a long sounding of the semitone *d#-e*. Cf. authentic pedalling in bar 149.

Bar 153 R.H. The second crotchet in the bar can be performed in three ways:
– as in the main text without the arpeggio;
– as in the main text with the arpeggio (c^2 simultaneously with the L.H. octave);
– in the version given in the variant.

p. 17   *Bar 169* R.H. The interpretation of the fingering added by Chopin in one of the pupil's copies poses certain difficulties. The most

probable deciphering:  seems to suggest that Chopin had in mind a triple, simultaneous striking with two fingers. This type of exceptional expressive fingering appears possibly also in *Mazurka in A minor* op. 59, no. 1, bar 25.

Bar 174 R.H. The trill composed of five notes sounds better; it can be also played as a mordent.

Bar 177 and 532 R.H. The fact that Chopin placed the marking *staccato* more or less in the middle of the chromatic scale probably means that few of its first notes should be performed *legato*, and that the articulation should be gradually changed so that several last notes are played distinctly *staccato*.

p. 18   *Bar 185 and 540* L.H. The last chord in these bars could be executed in a differentiated form (three notes in bar 185, four notes in bar 540) or in a form rendered uniform (three notes in both bars or four notes in both bars). See: *Source Commentary*.

p. 20

Bars 227-229 and analogous L.H. In these bars, a particularly beautiful effect is produced by the application of a "harmonic legato" (fingers sustain components of the harmony):

Such execution could be suggested by the marking *legato,* written at the beginning of the section in E major (bar 222). The employment of this performing device, much liked by Chopin, in the whole section (to bar 274) is indicated also by additional crotchet stems in bar 234 and 250-251.
Analogously in bars 578-580.

p. 21

Bar 250 R.H. The editors recommend the following solution of the grace-notes:

Bar 253 R.H. The way, preserved in our edition, in which seven octaves of the melody are arranged in relation to six quavers in the accompaniment suggests the following rhythmic division: [rhythmic notation].

Nonetheless, other groupings, e. g. the septolet: [rhythmic notation] cannot be excluded (cf. *Source Commentary*).
In the opinion of the editors, the way in which the notes in both hands were vertically aligned together with the marking *stretto* above the R.H. in the second half of the bar means that Chopin's intention was free R.H. r u b a t o against the background of the regular L.H., with a slight acceleration of the melody in octaves prior to the end of the bar.

Bar 255 and 257 In accordance with the sign added by Chopin in the pupil's copy, the grace-note in bar 255 should be struck together with the bass note. The grace-note in bar 257 can be played similarly.

p. 23

Bar 284 Markings *fz* refer to whole chords, and thus to grace-notes and to quavers played with the fifth fingers of both hands. The dynamic proportion, however, should be chosen in such a way so that the rhythm of the figuration is defined by quavers and not by grace-notes.

p. 26

Bars 329-332 and 667-670 In the opinion of the editors, signs *tr* occurring in the notation of the R.H. part mean that the whole combination of the trill and tremolando could be performed not only by means of semiquavers, but also freely, with a density adapted to the accepted tempo of this fragment and the execution skills of the player. The ending: [notation]

The L.H. trill (bars 331-332 and 669-670) should be started from the upper note.

p. 27

Bar 390 R.H. The turn should begin with the main note d^3.

p. 28

Bar 401 R.H. The beginning of the trill: $f\#^1$ simultaneously with d in the L.H. [notation]

Bars 404-406 R.H. The beginnings of trills – as in bar 401. In order to render possible an unhampered execution of the trills the lower voice can be partially taken into L.H.:

or

Analogously in next bars.

p. 31

Bars 449-450 and 453-454 R.H. Chopin's fingering is comfortable only for larger hands. The solution proposed by the editors can be additionally facilitated by the left hand striking the lower notes of the octaves on the second and third beat in bar 449 and at the beginning of bar 450. Analogously in bars 453-454.

p. 33

Bars 478-480 Signs [※] at the beginning of bar 479 and 480 define the earliest and last moment when, in the editors' opinion, the pedal depressed at the beginning of bar 478 can be changed for the first time.

p. 38

Bar 583 R.H. In the version given in the footnote (possibly mistaken – cf. main text and *Source Commentary*) the rhythm could be understood as:  or for the *ossia* version as:

p. 39

Bar 603 R.H. The way of aligning the triplet notes below the quintuplet, found in the sources and recreated in our edition, may correspond to the execution intended by Chopin, in which the second and third quaver of the lower note are sounded simultaneously with the third and fifth semiquaver of the quintuplet. In the opinion of the editors, it is also possible to arpeggiate some of the two-note chords, which is technically easier for smaller hands:  or

The latter solution is closest to precise rhythmic division (such a division is suggested by the script used in a similar figuration in *Fantasia in A* op. 13, bar 159). Cf. *Source Commentary*.

Bar 605 R.H. The first note of the arpeggio should be struck simultaneously with $c\#$ in the L.H.

Bar 607 and 609 R.H. The authentic graphic form of the grace-notes is uncertain (see: *Source Commentary*) so that we do not know what a rhythmic value Chopin foresaw for them. According to the editors, it would be most suitable to execute the grace-notes as semiquavers, but free realisations in longer values (even up to a crotchet) are also possible.

Bar 611 R.H. The rhythmic solution of the third beat:

The trill should be started from the main note.

Bar 614 R.H. The beginning of the trill as in bar 401 ($f\#^1$ together with B in the L.H.).

p. 40

Bar 621 and following L.H. The editors recommend the following rhythmic solution for the trills: [notation].

p. 41

Bar 654 The coordination mentioned in the footnote might prove necessary when the accompaniment is played – by the orchestra or the second piano—using a text other than the *National Edition* (cf. *Source Commentary*).

p. 42

Bars 661-662 R.H. Facilitation:

II. Romance. Larghetto

In this whole movement the R.H. arpeggios should be played so that their lowest note is sounded simultaneously with a corresponding L.H. note.

p. 43   *Bar 14* R.H. It is best to sound grace-note b^1 simultaneously with *a* in the L.H.

Bar 23 R.H. Grace-note $d\#^1$ should be played simultaneously with *B* in the L.H.

p. 44   *Bar 29* R.H. While deciding to opt for the *ossia* variant it is necessary to accentuate the $f\#\#^2$ note in the chord so as not to obliterate melodic progression $f\#^2$-$f\#\#^2$-$g\#^2$.

Bar 33, 48, 66, 82 and 90 R.H. $\boldsymbol{tr} = \sim\!\sim$

p. 46   *Bar 54* R.H. The execution of grace-note $g\#^1$ simultaneously with the third e-$g\#^1$ in the L.H. is more in keeping with the style.

Bar 55 R.H. Execution of the trill:

Bars 58-61 R.H. The versions given above the main text, and marked with numbers 1-3, correspond to Chopin's variants added in three pupils' copies of the *Concerto*. This fact compels the performer to select a version which he finds most suitable both musically and from the viewpoint of execution. The following remarks might prove useful for making the decision:
– the m a i n t e x t remains the basic and most certain version;
– the way in which the notes in the variant are arranged in relation to L.H. does not always have to strictly correspond to the synchronisation of both hands; this pertains predominantly to the repeated notes $c\#^3$ in variants 1 and 2, where the moment of beginning and ending those repetitions, their tempo and even number could, in the editors' opinion, be subjected to certain oscillations;
– the record in bar 61 (variant 1) could be regarded as incomplete (a sketch?, a scheme?, a beginning?); this is why it appears permissible to replace it with the arpeggio given at the bottom of the page;
– the alternative placings of variant 3 (in bar 59 and 61) exclude each other; its performance in both these bars is thus u n a c-c e p t a b l e.

p. 49   *Bar 98* R.H. It is best to begin the turn from the main note.

Bars 101-103 The editors propose the following pedalling :

III. Rondo. Vivace

In the majority of situations – bar 40, 170-177 and analogous – d o u b l e g r a c e - n o t e s should be started on the downbeat (according to classical rules). Only grace-notes in bar 36 should be performed in an anticipatory manner (before the fourth quaver of the bar). In bar 59 and 287 both ways of realising grace-notes appear to be possible.

p. 52   *Bars 14-17* In the sources the sign %o placed in bar 14, gives no assurance when it is necessary to depress the pedal, executing only the solo part. The editors suggest to do it in the beginning of bar 17. Similarly, it is not certain whether *p* in bar 15 pertains also to the solo part, which starts in the following bar.

Bar 20 and analog. In accordance with the mark added by Chopin in a pupil's copy, the second grace-note in bar 20 should be sounded together with the chord in the L.H. This pertains also to all analogous passages.

p. 54   *Bars 60-63 and 288-291* The application of the variant and the taking into consideration of other slight differences in the marking of both four bar sections (slurring, agogics) is left to the taste of the performer. In the opinion of the editors, the phrasing could be emphasised in the following manner, which is not contrary to the original script:

p. 55   *Bars 91-92* The placing of the marking *a tempo* already in bar 91, and thus half a bar earlier than in analogous bar 52 and 320, could be an effect intentionally introduced by Chopin or an accidental imprecision of the record. The decision is left to the performer.

Bars 96-97 R.H. In order not to undermine the rhythmic outline of the theme it is best to perform the grace-notes in an anticipatory manner.

p. 56   *Bar 129, 133, 137 and 141* R.H. The first semiquaver on the second quaver of the bar could be taken into L.H.

Bar 139 The coordination mentioned in the footnote might prove necessary when the accompaniment is played – by the orchestra or the second piano – using a text other than the *National Edition* (cf. *Source Commentary*).

p. 59   *Bars 212-213 and 216-217* Chopin's fingering of the first semiquaver triplet (inscribed in bar 216) could refer both to the right and left hand. The performer can choose a solution more suitable for him.

p. 62   *Bars 272-280* In the opinion of the editors, the markings *a tempo* in bar 272 and 280 have different meanings:
– the first restores the tempo in an apparently indecisive manner, just as indecisive as the theme itself, which appears in an unexpected E♭-major key, against the background of a second inversion chord, *dolcissimo* and with a more delicate accompaniment; the tempo in bars 272-279 should thus be slightly slower than the basic one;
– the second marking accompanies an already decisive (*f*!) return of the theme in the basic E major key; therefore, the basic tempo of the whole third movement of the *Concerto* returns in bar 280.
The acceptance of the above suggestions and the degree of the eventual differentiation of the tempi are left to the performer.

p. 72   *Bars 516-518* The rhythmic record of the final E-major scale seems to be conventional. The editors recommend the following rhythmic division, guaranteeing an even performance of the whole scale:

Bars 518-520 According to the editors, the whole ending (from the last chord in bar 518) could be included into the solo part.

Jan Ekier
Paweł Kamiński

SOURCE COMMENTARY /ABRIDGED/

Introductory comments

The following commentary pertains to the piano part, encompassing, apart from the solo part, also Chopin's piano reduction of the orchestral fragments. The commentary sets out in an abridged form the principles of editing the musical text and discusses the most important discrepancies between the authentic sources; furthermore, it draws attention to departures from the authentic text which are most frequently encountered in the collected editions of Chopin's music compiled after his death.

A commentary concerning the whole orchestra part is added to the score of the *Concerto*.

A separately published *Source Commentary* contains a detailed description of the sources, their filiation, justification of the choice of primary sources, a thorough presentation of the differences between them and a reproduction of characteristic fragments.

Abbreviations: R.H. – right hand, L.H. – left hand. The sign → symbolises a connection between sources; it should be read "and... based on it".

Remark to the third edition

The present edition takes into account few additional sources, i.a. another pupil's copy with Chopin's fingering in the 1st movement of the *Concerto*.

Concerto in E minor Op. 11

Sources

[A]   There is no extant autograph of the score.

A^{Tut}   Autograph of the opening *Tutti* (first movement, bars 1-138) in a version for one piano (private collection, photocopy in the Chopin Society in Warsaw). **A**^{Tut} was prepared as a supplement for the basis of the first French edition.

MFr^{orch} – manuscript of Auguste Franchomme containing the reduction of the orchestra part of the second and third movement of the *Concerto* (Bibliothèque Nationale, Paris), most likely prepared upon the basis of [**A**]. In longer fragments, marked as *Tutti*, played by the orchestra itself, Franchomme probably copied the original edition of Chopin's piano reduction found in [**A**].

MFr^w   Manuscript of Auguste Franchomme containing the piano reduction of the wind instruments in the second and third movement of the *Concerto* (Bibliothèque Nationale, Paris), made – similarly to **MFr**^{orch} – probably upon the basis of [**A**]. It includes several directives describing the instrumentation.

MFr   = **MFr**^{orch} and **MFr**^w. The score emerging from the two Franchomme manuscripts differs in numerous details from the score composed of parts in first French edition, testifying to changes conducted in the course of the preparation of that edition.

FE   First French edition, M. Schlesinger (M. S. 1409), Paris June 1833, encompassing the *Concerto* in the version for one piano and orchestral parts. The opening fragment of the piano part in **FE** is based on **A**^{Tut}, and in further sections probably on [**A**], and was corrected by Chopin at least twice. Nonetheless, it contains multiple imprecision in the notation of the accidentals and the performance markings (slurs, accents, *staccato* markings) as well as a number of errors. It is also characteristic that fragments of the orchestra part, which can be recreated upon the basis of the piano part (predominantly the so-called *Tutti*) differ in numerous details from the version following from the orchestral parts. There are copies of **FE** with different prices and other details of the cover, originating from impressions published by Brandus, the successor of Schlesinger.

FE^{piano}, **FE**^{orch} – the piano part and orchestral parts in **FE**; these symbols are applied only in those cases when the use of '**FE**' alone could lead to vagueness.

FED, **FE**S, **FE**Fo, **FE**H – pupils' copies of **FE**^{piano} with annotations made by Chopin, containing fingering, performance directives, variants and corrections of printing errors:

FED – copy from the collection belonging to Chopin's pupil Camille Dubois (Bibliothèque Nationale, Paris).

FES – copy from the collection belonging to Chopin's pupil Jane Stirling (Bibliothèque Nationale, Paris).

FEFo – copy with Chopin's dedication to his pupil Adèle Forest (Pierpont Morgan Library, New York).

FEH – copy possibly belonging to Chopin's pupil Caroline Hartmann, and part of a collection presumably completed by another of his pupils, Joseph Schiffmacher (private collections[1]) – a suggestion made by J. J. Eigeldinger, *Chopin: Pianist and Teacher As Seen by his Pupils* Cambridge 1988. Some of the annotations contained therein (variants, certain corrections of errors and some of the fingering) were certainly, or with a great dose of probability, added by the composer, while others, i. a. most of the fingering, were added in a different handwriting.

FEJ   Copy of **FE**^{piano} from the collection belonging to Chopin's sister Ludwika Jędrzejewiczowa (the F. Chopin Society, Warsaw). It contains corrections, possibly made by Chopin, of several most glaring errors committed by the engraver.

GE1   First German edition, Fr. Kistner (1020.1021.1022), Leipzig September 1833, including the *Concerto* in the version for one piano and orchestral parts. **GE**1 is most probably based on a proof copy of **FE**, which does not take into consideration the final corrections made by Chopin. It contains traces of a very detailed revision by the publisher, in most cases carried out only in the course of printing, as well as a number of errors. Some of the introduced changes (e. g. first movement, bar 391, 393, 453; third movement, bar 139) have been heretofore regarded as authentic, since they occur in the overwhelming majority of the later collected editions. Nonetheless, the absence of a distinct confirmation of Chopin's participation in the proofreading of **GE**1 renders the authenticity of this edition extremely doubtful, as evidenced by the following arguments:
– the correspondence between the publishers, Schlesinger in Paris and Kistner in Leipzig, demonstrates that Chopin established direct contact only with the Parisian publisher, who then offered the purchased compositions to his colleague in Leipzig; the introduction of improvements in **GE**1 while bypassing the main Parisian contracting party would have been an unwise move for a composer starting to issue his works in France;
– apart from changes which could be regarded as made by Chopin, **GE**1 contains also others, evidently mistaken, which cannot be in any way ascribed to Chopin (e.g. 1st movt, bar 190, 632).

GE2   Corrected reprint of the **GE**1, presumably from 1834-1837, containing several corrections, not always apt (e.g. 1st movt, bar 416). There are copies of **GE**1 with different details of the cover, i.a. the price.

GE3   Second German edition of the version for one piano (bearing an additional plate number 2340) from 1858, containing numerous further adjustments, including arbitrary changes, and several errors. The editors of the *National Edition* are not aware of the existence of differentiated impressions of the orchestral material of **GE**.

GE   = **GE**1, **GE**2 and **GE**3.

GE^{piano}, **GE**^{orch} – the piano part and orchestral parts of **GE** (analogously to **FE**^{piano}, **FE**^{orch}).

EE   First English edition of the version for one piano, Wessel & C° (W & C° N° 1086), London, May 1834, based most probably on **FE**. According to information found on the cover, **EE** was "edited and with fingering by" Julian Fontana. Chopin did not participate in the production of **EE**. The editors of the *National Edition* failed to locate a copy of the orchestral parts of **EE**; thus it is most likely that – as in the case of the *Concerto in F minor*, Op. 21 – the orchestral material was not printed in **EE**.

Mi   Edition prepared by Chopin's pupil Karol Mikuli (Kistner, Leipzig 1879), including two authentic variants.

---

[1] The editors of the National Edition wish warmly to thank Mr. Jan M. **Huizing**, Assen, for making a photocopy of this source available.

Editorial principles for the solo part
We accept as our basis **FE** as the only indubitably authentic source, and take into consideration Chopin's annotations in **FE**D, **FE**S **FE**Fo and those annotations in **FE**H, whose graphological features and contents indicate with great probability Chopin's handwriting (this restriction pertains especially to the fingering). We also cite variants found in **Mi**.
Inconsistent slurring and other articulation markings have been put into order by keeping in mind obvious analogies and knowledge about Chopin's habits, documented in other compositions, as well as typical alterations found in the original editions. In order not to overburden the text, in obvious situations we do not apply brackets. In those cases where differentiation could correspond to Chopin's intentions we leave the source versions.
In several places the graphic form and manner of performing individual grace-notes give rise to doubts. A comparison of their script in autographs from this period in Chopin's oeuvre proves that forms other than crossed quavers were applied only exceptionally. All problematic places are discussed in commentaries to appropriate bars.
We try to retain the distinction between long and short accents characteristic of Chopin. It is not always possible to meticulously recreate the composer's intentions owing to the absence of an autograph and visible imprecision in the first editions (this holds true also for the allocation of accents to the right or left hand).

I. Allegro maestoso

The reduction of the orchestra part

p. 13   *Beginning* In **A**^{Tut} there is no marking of the metronomic tempo. Chopin added it in the proofs of **FE** (→**GE**,**EE**).

Bars 13-15 R.H. We give the octave doubling according to **A**^{Tut} (→**FE**^{piano}→**GE**^{piano},**EE**). Here, **FE**^{orch} (→**GE**^{orch}) has the first flute (bar 13), flutes in unison (bar 14) and the first bassoon (bars 14-15).

Bar 14 and 18 In accordance with **A**^{Tut} (→**FE**^{piano}→**GE**^{piano},**EE**) we give only the melodic voice. **FE**^{orch} (→**GE**^{orch}) features an additional harmonic background of the strings, as in bar 499 and 503.

Bar 25, 29 and 30 R.H. We give dotted rhythms on the last crotchets according to **A**^{Tut} (→**FE**^{piano}→**GE**^{piano},**EE**). Here, **FE**^{orch} (→**GE**^{orch}) has equal quavers (Vni I).

Bar 33 L.H. We give the *F#-f#* octave at the beginning of the bar according to **A**^{Tut} (→**FE**^{piano}→**GE**^{piano},**EE**). Here, **FE**^{orch} (→**GE**^{orch}) has: [musical notation] (Vc. and Cb.)

Bars 39-40 R.H. The lowest note in the chords on the fifth and sixth quaver in **A**^{Tut} is *d²*. In the proofs of **FE** (→**GE**,**EE**) they were changed – probably by Chopin – to *c²* and *b¹*.

Bar 42 R.H. In **A**^{Tut} the first two quavers are *b¹-e²-g²* and *b¹-b²*. The notes *g¹* and *g²* were added – probably by Chopin – in the proofs of **FE** (→**GE**,**EE**).

p. 14   *Bars 62-63 and 70-71* L.H. We give the accompaniment according to **A**^{Tut} (→**FE**^{piano}→**GE**^{piano},**EE**). In **FE**^{orch} (→**GE**^{orch}) the bass line of the cellos begins with a crotchet upbeat in bar 62 and 70.

p. 15   *Bar 96* L.H. We give the note *A* as the fundamental bass note for the whole bar in accordance with **A**^{Tut} (→**FE**^{piano},**EE**). **FE**^{orch} (→**GE**^{orch}) has *B* (Vc. and Cb.) throughout the first four quavers. This is the version introduced also in **GE**^{piano}.

Bars 123-125 L.H. In **A**^{Tut} there are no ties sustaining *e*.

Bar 134 R.H. In **A**^{Tut} the note *a* at the beginning of the bar has the value of a dotted minim, and is probably not repeated on the third crotchet (precise deciphering is impossible owing to the deletions and erasing visible in this bar in the photocopy available to the editors of the *National Edition*). In **FE** (→**GE**,**EE**) the note *a*

occurs only on the third crotchet. The absence of *a* at the beginning of the bar is undoubtedly the result of a misunderstanding during the proofreading or deciphering of **A**^{Tut}. We give the version linking the most certain elements of the sources.

Bar 135 L.H. In **A**^{Tut} there is no lower *E*.

The solo part

p. 16   *Bar 149* R.H. The 8 last notes in **FE** (→**GE**1) are mistakenly beamed as semiquavers. The suitable correction was written into **FE**J.

Bar 153 R.H. The arpeggio on the second beat is found in **Mi**; most probably, it was added by Chopin in one of the pupil's copies, which the editor of this edition examined. The version given in the variant also comes from **Mi,** where it was described as "execution according to Chopin".

p. 17   *Bar 162* R.H. On the first beat both the pitches and the rhythmic values of the notes give rise to doubts. **FE** has a version with an obvious rhythmic error: [musical notation]. Presumably, this mistake was the outcome of cancellations in [A], making it difficult for the engraver to properly decipher the text; the proof copy also could have contained corrections. In all likelihood, they also caused the error in the pitch record (as indicated by Chopin's correction in **FE**D). **GE** includes a possibly arbitrary correction of the rhythm: [musical notation]. We may merely surmise the origin of the **EE** version [musical notation], although nothing indicates that it could have corresponded to Chopin's ultimate intention.
We give the only fully authentic version corrected by Chopin in **FE**D both as regards rhythm (the deletion of the dot prolonging the first quaver) and melody (a change of the second and third note from *b¹-a¹* to *a¹-g¹*). This version is concurrent with the one in analogous bar 517, which does not produce any doubts.

p. 18   *Bar 168 and 523* R.H. **GE** contains the following, possibly original notation of the second beat: [musical notation]

Bar 169 R.H. The fingering, discussed in the *Performance Commentary*, difficult to decipher and with an unclear meaning, is added to **FE**D.

Bar 177 and 532 R.H. Some of the later collected editions arbitrarily removed the slur encompassing this bar and shifted the *staccato* marking to the beginning of the bar. See: *Performance Commentary*.

Bar 185 and 540 L.H. In the sources, the chord on the last beat has three notes in bar 185 and four in bar 540. We should not exclude the possibility that this is the result of an imprecise deciphering of [A], and that Chopin intended both passages to have an identical text. Some of the later collected editions introduced suitable changes by removing *b* from bar 540 or adding it in bar 185. Cf. *Performance Commentary*.

Bar 190 R.H. In **GE**1 (→**GE**2) ♮ was mistakenly added before the eighth semiquaver.

p. 19   *Bar 195* L.H. In the first chord **GE** erroneously has *e¹* instead of *g¹*.

Bars 197-200 and 556-557 R.H. In **FE** (→**EE**,**GE**1 →**GE**2) the slurs are not broken above the rests. This is probably a remnant of the original version of phrasing those bars (with equal semiquavers). In **FE**D the necessity of separating the first two notes from the remaining ones was confirmed by Chopin with pencilled marking.

Bars 197-198, 201-202 and analog. L.H. Some of the later collected editions arbitrarily rendered uniform the versions of those bars, adding ties sustaining *c#¹* in bars 197-198 and *f#¹* in bars 201-202, or removing them from bars 552-553 and 556-557.

p. 20
Bar 222 R.H. The main text comes from **FE** (→**EE**). The variant is probably the original version occurring in **GE**.

p. 21
Bar 234 L.H. The sources do not have *G#* on the fifth quaver. A corresponding note is found, however, in all four analogous places, and at least in two (bar 226 and 585) it was added at the time of printing **FE**. In this situation, it is most likely that in the discussed bar Chopin left the uncorrected original version due to inattention – the omission of one of several recurring fragments while introducing corrections is one of his most frequent mistakes.

Bar 236 R.H. The wedges were added in **FE**D.

Bar 238 R.H. In **GE**3 the tie sustaining *d#¹* was removed (overlooked?).

Bars 238-239 and 242-243 L.H. In **GE** bars 238-239 do not have a tie sustaining *B*. In some of the later collected editions this error was repeated also in bars 242-243.

Bar 250 R.H. In **FE** the grace-notes have the form of small crotchets. Since in this particular context such a form of the grace-notes is unjustified, we recognise it as an engraver's error (often encountered, especially in the earlier impressions of **FE**). We give the form of crossed quavers, most frequently used by Chopin (similar changes were made in **GE** and **EE**).

Bar 253 R.H. **FE** (→**GE**,**EE**) does not have any figure defining the rhythmic shape of the group of seven quavers. The arrangement of the notes in **FE** in relation to the left hand is not conclusive, since this edition contains quite frequent evident errors (e. g. bar 519, second movement, bar 23, third movement, bar 475; cf. also comments to *Nocturne in B♭ minor* op. 9 no. 1, bar 73 and 75). See: *Performance Commentary*.

Bar 255 and 257 R.H. We give the grace-notes in the form of uncrossed quavers, as in **FE** (→**EE**). Nonetheless, we cannot exclude the imprecision of the engraver of **FE** – cf. commentary to bar 250, 577, 607 and 609. In **GE** both those and all other grace-notes have the form of crossed quavers. Cf. *Performance Commentary*.

Bar 255 and 403 In **FE**D Chopin marked a simultaneous striking of the grace note with the bass note.

p. 22
Bars 264-265 R.H. In **FE** (→**GE**,**EE**) the slur is uninterrupted. We take into consideration the correction of the phrasing added by Chopin in **FE**D.

Bar 275 In **FE** the *f̷z* sign is placed above the rest in L.H. on the second quaver of the bar, so that it is not quite clear whether it refers to the chord at the beginning of the bar or the stroke commencing the semiquaver figurations. We accept the second possibility, much more probable from the viewpoint both of the sources and the music:
– a number of graphic aspects of the notation in **FE** links this sign with the beginning of the second beat; this is also the way its location was understood in **GE** and **EE**;
– the beginning of a similar semiquaver figure in bar 277 is also accented.

p. 23
Bars 281-282 The possibility of *ritenuto* being misplaced in bar 281 in **FE** (→**EE**,**GE**1→**GE**2) is the result of the following premises:
– by accepting the natural assumption that *ritenuto* is to last until *risoluto* in bar 283 (cf. bars 407-408) we would receive an almost one-and-a-half bar-long slowing down, the longest among those marked by Chopin in this movement and unjustified after a barely eight-bar prelude to the final figurate part of the exposition;
– the third crotchet in bar 281 and the second one in bar 282 are graphically identical, which could have been the reason for the engraver's error.

Bar 288 R.H. The fourth semiquaver in **FE** (→**EE**) is *b³* and not *a³* (in **GE**1 & **GE**2 it is *b²*, since these editions overlooked the *8ᵛᵃ* sign

used in the notation of **FE**). A comparison with bar 304, as well as 287 and 303 indicates the probable error in the first editions.

Bar 290 R.H. The tenth semiquaver in **FE** (→**GE**1) is *d#²*. This obvious mistake – cf. bar 289 and 305-306 – was corrected in **FE**D. **EE** and **GE**2 (→**GE**3) also contain the proper version.

p. 24
Bars 296-297 and 312-313 R.H. **FE** (→**GE**) first (bars 296-297) has a tie sustaining *c#²*, and then (bar 313) a slur running from *c#²* to *b¹*. Owing to the identical musical and execution context of both those passages such a differentiation seems unjustified; this is the reason why we accept that the slur in bar 313 was written mistakenly (this type of an error, consisting of placing ties on the opposite side of the notes, in this case, to the right instead of the left of *c#²* in bar 313, occurs quite often in prints from the period, e. g. in *Scherzo in B♭ minor* op. 31, bars 265-266 and *in E,* op. 54, bars 480-481). The version with *c#²* sustained in both passages is found in **EE**.

Bar 298 L.H. In **FE**D the fingering number was written above note *b*. It is quite possible, however, that it should be referred to *d#¹* in the R.H.

Bar 308 L.H. The sixth semiquaver in **FE** is *e*. The indubitable mistake is evidenced by a comparison with analogous bar 292 and similarly constructed adjoining bars. A handwritten correction of *e* into *c#* is visible in **FE**H; **GE** and **EE** also have the proper version.

p. 25
Bar 317 R.H. In some of the later collected editions the semiquaver fifth from the end was arbitrarily changed from *a²* to *a#²*. R.H. The last semiquaver in **GE** is *b³*. This is most probably an error: *d#⁴* occurring in **FE** (→**EE**) creates together with the preceding note an interval of a sixth, as in analogous bars 315-316, and has not been changed in any of the pupils' copies.

Bar 321 L.H. At the end of the bar **GE** and **EE** have – probably mistakenly – the octave *B-b* (cf. previous bars).

p. 26
Bar 326 R.H. The eighth semiquaver in **FE** is erroneously *b#²*.

Bars 329-332 and 667-670 R.H. Some of the later collected editions arbitrarily changed the notation in these bars. In bars 329-332 minims *f#³*, with the sign of a trill, were removed, and notes comprising the trill were added to the components of the tremolando – *g#³* to *b³*, and *f#³* to the second *a²-b²*. Bars 667-670 were changed analogously. Such a modified script mistakenly enjoins that this figure be played in semiquavers. Cf. commentary to bars 667-670 and *Performance Commentary*.

The reduction of the orchestra part

p. 27
Bars 356-359 At the end of the bars **GE**ᵖⁱᵃⁿᵒ has two quavers instead of a dotted rhythm. This version, probably mistaken, occurred initially also in **FE**ᵖⁱᵃⁿᵒ, where, however, it was corrected by Chopin in the last phase of the proofreading.

Bar 364 R.H. **FE** (→**EE**) mistakenly has *g²* as the lower note of the chord on the third quaver.

Bar 378 L.H. At the end of the bar **FE**ᵖⁱᵃⁿᵒ (→**EE**) has the crotchet *A*. Chopin corrected this error in **FE**D. **FE**ᵒʳᶜʰ and **GE** contain the proper version.

Bar 385 R.H. At the beginning of the bar in **GE**ᵖⁱᵃⁿᵒ there is no third *c¹-e¹*, ending the last phrase of the *Tutti* section.

The solo part

Bar 385 R.H. **FE** (→**EE**) has no ♮ prior to the last note. It was probably overlooked – this type of an omission of accidentals next to notes belonging to the key fixed in a given passage belongs to errors most frequently committed by Chopin. The sign was supplemented in **FE**H; **GE** also contains the correct version.

Bar 390 R.H. The sources overlooked ♯ under the sign of the turn.

Bar 391 R.H. The first note of the melody in **FE** (→**EE**) is *g¹*. The fact that this is not an error is testified by an additional, sweeping slur *f³-g¹* (apart from the already printed one), added by Chopin in **FE**D. At the time of printing **GE**1 this note was transferred an octave higher. Since there are no arguments which would confirm the authenticity of the changes made in **GE**, we do not take this version into consideration. The melodic interval joined with the slur, and exceeding the span of an average hand, is an expressive device applied upon several occasions by Chopin (cf., e. g. mov. II, bars 65-66, or *Nocturne in B*, op. 62 no. 1, bars 88-89).

Bar 393 R.H. The rhythm with a quaver at the beginning of the motif, given by us, occurs in **FE** (→**EE**). This version was changed in **GE** (at the time of printing **GE**1) into the one found in analogous bars (e. g. 385, 389), with the first *e²* having the value of a semiquaver. Here, the occurrence of this frequently repeated motif in a slightly altered rhythmic form, as in the authentic **FE** version, is justified by the further development of the phrase – cf. corresponding motif in bar 395.

p. 28 *Bar 401* R.H. Prior to the first grace-note of the bar **FE**H contains an added sign in the shape of a diagonal cross. It can be interpreted as ✕, raising *f♯¹* to *f♯♯¹* at the beginning, and, it cannot be excluded, at the end of the trill. However, we do not take these possibilities into consideration in the form of variants since the meaning of this sign is uncertain (Chopin used similar crosses to mark passages, which had been discussed during lessons – this particular pupil's copy and others contain numerous such signs).

Bar 402 R.H. The first eight notes in **FE** are probably mistakenly joined with a semiquaver beam.

Bar 405 L.H. The third quaver in the sources does not have the note *c¹*. In situations of this sort it is very difficult to say whether in Chopin's manuscripts the note placed on a ledger line occurs in a chord, and thus it is very likely that the engraver overlooked the note in question (cf. bar 404 and 406).

p. 29 *Bar 412* L.H. The fingering number in **FE**D was added above the note *f¹*. It is also possible that it should be referred to *g♯¹* in the R.H.

Bar 415 Some of the later collected editions arbitrarily changed notes *e¹* and *e³* to *f¹* and *f³* on the first beat, and *e²* to *f²* on the second beat.

Bar 416 R.H. In **GE**2 (→**GE**3) the fifth *e¹-b¹*, which occurs in **FE** (→**GE**1,**EE**), was altered to the fourth *e¹-a¹*. It would be difficult to assume that this change concurs with Chopin's intentions, since *e¹-b¹* corresponds to *b¹* in the accompanying voice of the first violins.

Bars 416-423 and 440-447 R.H. In the sources, we encounter, alongside the most frequent script ♩♫♫ (accepted by us for all the figures) the following notation: ♫♫♩, possibly original or simplified for graphic purposes. This is the way in which the second figure in bar 419 and 421, the second and third figure in bar 423, and both figures in bars 442-443 are recorded.

p. 30 *Bars 435-436* R.H. In **GE**3 both *f♯* are arbitrarily tied over bar line.

Bar 436 R.H. In **GE**3 the note *f♯¹* was overlooked (removed?) in the chord at the beginning of the bar.

p. 31 *Bar 453* R.H. The first semiquaver in **FE** (→**EE**) is *f♯* alone, while **GE** has the octave *f♯-f♯¹*. A comparison with analogous bar 449 could seem to indicate the correctness of the **GE** version. The differentiation of those bars is, however, justified by a link, different in each of those passages, with the preceding figuration:

– the upper *g♯¹* in the octave in bar 449 continues the line of *a♯¹*, the penultimate semiquaver in bar 448; the notes *c♯¹* and *f♯¹*, joint for the chords in both bars, make it possible to retain the unchanged position of the hand;
– in bar 453 the direct continuation of *b¹* from the previous bar is unnecessary, since this is a note joint for the chords in those bars; from the viewpoint of execution, the single *f♯* in bar 453 is connected in a natural manner with the preceding passage thanks to the retained position of the first finger (making it possible to avoid the impression of a parallel shift of both hands); the fingering given by us is to be found in **FE**H.
It should be emphasized that the striking of the octaves in bar 453 is reinforced by accents, which do not appear until the second beat. Taking into consideration the above arguments and the fact that the authenticity of the changes made in **GE** remains unconfirmed we give only the **FE** edition.

p. 33 *Bars 477-478* L.H. The ties sustaining *B* and *f♯* have been presumably added in the last proofs of **FE** (→**EE**) since they are missing in **GE**.

Bar 486 In the sources, the solo part ends abruptly at the end of bar 485, because the entire bar 486, together with its first chord, is recorded in **FE** (→**GE,EE**) by means of small notes due to the fact that it belongs to the orchestra part. Since this is certainly a mistake, we add a natural ending to the figurations of the solo part.

The reduction of the orchestra part

p. 34 *Bar 498* R.H. Prior to the first chord **FE**^piano (→**EE**) has ♮ on the level of *b¹*. This is certainly an error – cf. chords in bar 502 as well as in bar 13 and 17; an eventual *b¹* would not require any sort of a sign. **FE**^orch (Ob., Cor., Vla) and **GE** contain *b♭¹*.
R.H. In the opening chord **GE**^piano has an additional *e²*. This note was removed, probably by Chopin, in the last proofs of **FE**^piano (→**EE**).

The solo part

p. 35 *Bar 530* R.H. **FE** (→**EE**) has no tie sustaining *c³*, probably an oversight.

Bar 533 L.H., The source version has distinct, in this context badly sounding parallel octaves *e-e¹* and *g-g¹*. Considering the absence of arguments in favour of a differentiation of those bars a comparison with analogous bar 178 indicates the possibility of a mistaken exchange of the notes by the engraver of **FE**. Mistakes of this type occurred in the first editions of Chopin's works (cf. commentary to *Prelude in B♭ minor* op. 28 no. 16, bar 2).

p. 36 *Bar 548-549* L.H. In **FE** (→**GE**) there is no tie sustaining *a¹*. Cf. bars 193-194. The tie was added in **EE**.

p. 37 *Bar 555* R.H. The last semiquaver in **FE** is mistakenly *e♯²*.

p. 38 *Bar 577* R.H. In **FE** the grace-note has the form of a small crotchet. As in bar 250 – see: commentary – we give it the form of a crossed quaver.
L.H. The main text comes from **FE** (→**GE,EE**). The sound of the fourth quaver, different than in all analogous bars (bar 226, 234, 250 and 585; cf. also bar 67, 73 and 89), could have been intended by Chopin, for example, in connection with a slightly differently delineated accompaniment line in the following bar. Since the engraver's error cannot be excluded, we give the version concurrent with the remaining bars in the variant.

Bar 583 R.H. The possibility that the **FE** (→**EE,GE**1 →**GE**2) version given at the bottom of the page could be mistaken is evidenced by the following arguments:
– r h y t h m i c – the record in the form of two groups of semiquavers marked with the figures 7 suggests that each of those groups corresponded to a well-defined metric unit (crotchet); this suggestion is confirmed by the rhythm of analogous bar 232;

– melodic – in this instance, septolets comprise a figurate variant of the motif, which appears in its basic rhythmic form as many as

twelve times:

The following script (Chopin used a similar one in *Concerto in F minor* op. 21, third movement, bar 27) illustrates the close connection between the two forms of the motif:

– the possibility that the engraver or Chopin himself overlooked the rest; Chopin made few mistakes of this type (cf. commentary to *Ballade in Ab* op. 47, bar 138), especially if he introduced corrections, which is quite probable in the discussed passages owing to the dynamic and articulation changes in relation to bar 232.

On the other hand, we cannot entirely reject the possibility that the purpose of the mentioned eventual changes in [A] was to shift by a quaver the moment of commencing the semiquaver figures; the notation in the sources, although unusual, does not contain an error. This version would comprise an original example of the Chopinesque *rubato*, a possibility favoured by the absence of corrections in pupil's copies.

The overwhelming majority of the later collected editions has the **GE**3 version, with the opening b^2 possessing the value of a crotchet. R.H. The *ossia* variant comes from **Mi**. The performance markings and fingering contained therein could have been added by the editor of this edition, and the openning crotchet value is taken

from **GE**3:

p. 39

Bar 587 L. H. We give the main text according to **FE** (→**GE,EE**). The variant in the footnote, analogous to bar 75 and 237, makes it possible to avoid hidden parallel octaves of leading notes $f\#$-$f\#^1$ to g-g^1. The probability of an engraver's error while deciphering the note with a distance of a third is considerable (cf., e. g. bar 290 and 308 in this movement and bar 73 and 108 in the second movement).

Bar 603 R.H. In some of the later collected editions the second and third note of the lower voice triplet are placed below the two last notes of the quintuplet, together creating octaves. This certainly does not correspond to Chopin's intentions; if the composer had such a performance in mind he would have probably written the figure as ♪♪♪♪. See: *Performance Commentary*.

Bar 607 R.H. In **FE** the note a^2 has the form of a small crotchet, albeit slightly larger than the one used in this edition for the grace-notes, and is placed above the minim d^2. This note is absent in **GE**, while **EE** contains the version given in our main text as the most probable conjecture of the **FE** version (cf. bar 609). Owing to the fact that Chopin's ultimate intention remains uncertain, we give the **GE** version, which could be authentic (original) in the variant. In this type of a context we encounter two possibilities in Chopin's works, cf., e. g. *Nocturne in G minor* op. 37 no. 1, bars 19-20 and 35-36.

Bar 607 and 609 R.H. In accordance with **FE** (→**EE**) we give grace-notes with the value of a crotchet, possibly intended by Chopin. A mistake made by the engraver is just as likely (see: commentary to bar 607 as well as to bar 250, 255, 257 and 577). In **GE** the grace-note in bar 609 has the form of a crossed quaver.

Bar 614 L.H. The sixth quaver in **EE** is probably mistakenly e.

Bars 618-619 R.H. One can doubt whether Chopin actually wanted to tie the a^1 demisemiquaver, which is suggested by the tie, visible in the sources, combining it with the crotchet in the next bar. In a similar melodic-rhythmic context, which appears upon numerous occasions in works by Chopin, the downbeat note is always struck (repeated) – cf., e. g. bars 220-221, 571-572, 606-609. This is the reason why it seems highly probable that in this case too Chopin's intention was to repeat a^1 at the beginning of bar 619. This conclusion is sustained in our opinion by the original version of that fragment, as revealed by an analysis of the visible

traces of corrections in **FE**: . One can

see that in spite of the tied a^1 the melody was not deprived of a note played on downbeat. The correction was most likely aimed at enhancing the expression by a dramatic appoggiatura:

 (cf. the commentary to bar 607). In

this situation, it seems almost certain that the tie of the original version was left here by inadvertence (this type of "partial" corrections, in which some elements to be removed were left behind – accidentally or in order to avoid an overcomplicated correcting – occurred in Chopin's works in several instances, e. g. the shorter slurs in R.H. in the third movement, bars 180-181, or the erroneous notes in *Scherzo in B minor* op. 20, bar 135 and 292).

Bar 620 R.H. The absence of an accidental before the fourth semiquaver in **FE** (→**EE,GE**1→**GE**2) is certainly an oversight – this type of figures, very frequent in Chopin's works, which describe the opening note in the manner of a turn, contain minor or major, but never augmented seconds. We add $\#$ as the most probable in this passage (cf., e. g. bar 220).

p. 40

Bar 632 R.H. **GE** mistakenly added $\natural$ before the sixth semiquaver.

Bar 636 R.H. In **FE** (→**EE,GE**1→**GE**2) $\#$ raising c^2 to $c\#^2$ is not found until before the fourth quaver of the lower voice. Chopin made this type of error upon several occasions (e. g. in *Mazurka in A minor* Dbop. 42B, bar 61 or *Etude in F* op. 10 no. 8, bar 43).

Bar 639 R.H. The fourth quaver of the lower voice in **GE** is erroneously b^2.

p. 41

Bar 654 L.H. At the beginning of the bar all the sources give fb as the fundamental bass note (the octave Fb-fb in the piano part and fb in the cello part). Some of the later collected editions arbitrarily changed the bass to f. Chopin left the unchanged octave with flats in all three pupil's copies containing annotations added in other places on this page.

Bar 658 L.H. Upon the basis of available sources it is impossible to ascertain whether Chopin decided to opt for one version of the first bass note, and if so then which one. **FE**^piano (→**GE,EE**) contains e, which Chopin left unchanged in **FE**D and **FE**H. Nonetheless, in **FE**^orch the cellos have eb^1; and in **FE**S there are flats pencilled in before the first chord, which resemble Chopin's hand.

p. 42

Bars 665-666 R.H. In those bars **FE**D has the following fingering, added probably by a pupil:

Bars 667-670 R.H. For the combination of the trill and tremolando we accept the notation which occurs in the sources in bars 329-332. In the discussed bars this figure is recorded in **FE** as

follows:

GE and **EE** basically recreated this script, correcting errors and imprecision: in bar 667 c^3 was changed to b^2 and missing pro-longation dots were supplemented. Moreover, the tremolando in bar 667 (**GE**) or in all the four bars (**EE**) was written out in semi-quavers.

Presumably, the above **FE** notation, in which the trill on $f\#^2$ ($f\#^3$) is doubled in the record of the tremolando, resulted from a sup-plementation of the original record (at the time of printing it), analogous to bars 329-332. The purpose of this change was probably to render precise the manner in which both elements of this figure should be combined. We cannot exclude the possibility that the introduction of this specific "performance commentary" was suggested to Chopin by, e. g. his publisher. See also: com-mentary to bars 329-332.

Bar 669 and 670 L.H. Some of the later collected editions arbit-rarily added minims b^1 to both $d\#^2$.

Bar 671 L.H. In **GE** the note c^2, which in **FE** (→**EE**) is printed smaller because it belongs to the orchestra part, mistakenly has a head of normal size; as a result, in the majority of the later col-lected editions it is included into the solo part.

II. Romance. Larghetto

The reduction of the orchestra part

p. 43

Bar 1 On the fourth beat **MFr**^{orch} has two quavers. This could be the original version, changed by Chopin in **FE**, or an error.

Bars 1-5 R.H. A slur above the whole phrase is to be found in **MFr**^{orch} as well as in the first violins part in **FE**^{orch} (→**GE**^{orch}). The absence of a slur in **FE**^{piano} (→**GE**^{piano},**EE**) could be, therefore, accidental.

The solo part

Bar 13 L.H. In the sources the first quaver in the upper voice is the sixth $g\#$-e^1 (our variant). It is most probable, however, that Chopin intended the note e^1 to be printed smaller, because it be-longs only to the orchestra. This hypothesis is supported by the following arguments:
– it is natural that the outline of the accompaniment is clearly de-lineated from the first figure; the initiation of the upper voice line on e^1 delays and hampers the shaping of the characteristic, un-dulating motif;
– the version without e^1, accepted by us in the main text, appears in analogous bar 54;
– upon several occasions the engraver granted certain notes an incorrect size in those passages where the solo part begins or ends, e. g. first movement, bar 486 and 671.

Bar 14 R.H. In **GE** the grace-note is mistakenly $d\#^2$.

Bar 16 and 57 R.H. In **FE** (→**GE**) there is no arpeggio sign be-fore the second chord. **EE** and some of the later collected edi-tions added a wavy line. It was certainly Chopin's intention that this chord be struck simultaneously with the use of the first finger to play the third $d\#^1$-$f\#^1$, as testified by:
– the fact that in the proofs of **FE** Chopin removed the arpeggio originally (mistakenly?) printed in bar 16; this edition contains visible traces of such an operation;
– the number 1 added prior to this third in both bars in the last proofs of **FE** (it is absent in **GE**).
A similar chord, also without an arpeggio and with the simultane-ous sounding of the minor third on the black keys with the first finger, marked by Chopin with bracket, occurs in *Prélude in A* op. 28 no. 7.

Bar 21 R.H. Chopin added the *staccato* dots above the last two quavers in **FE**D.

p. 44

Bar 29 R.H. The variant comes from **FE**H. The leading of the melody within the wider chords, frequently with the span of a ninth between extreme notes, belongs to characteristic com-position-execution devices applied by Chopin (cf., e. g. *Ballade in G minor* op. 23, bar 114 and 174, *Prélude in F#*, op. 28 no. 13, bars 30-32, *Sonata in Bb minor* op. 35, third movement, bars 19-20, *Prélude in C# minor* op. 45, bar 79).

Bar 39 and 41 R.H. In **FE** (→**GE**1) there is no ♮ restoring e^2 in the last third on the third beat. In **FE**S it was added in bar 39. Chopin frequently made mistakes of this type in melodic lines led in thirds – cf., e. g. bar 88 and 90 in this movement as well as *Mazurka in E* op. 6 no. 3, bar 11, 13 and analogous.

p. 45

Bar 42 R.H. **FE** has ♮ prior to the tenth semiquaver ($a\#^2$). This obvious engraver's error was corrected in **FE**S, **FE**J and **FE**H.

Bar 43 R.H. None of the first editions has ✕ raising $c\#^2$ to $c\#\#^2$ on the fourth third nor ♯ restoring $c\#^2$ on the last quaver of the sec-ond triplet. This is probably yet another Chopin's oversight (cf. commentary to bar 39, 41) since there are no arguments in fa-vour of differentiating this passage in relation to analogous bar 39, 41 and 88, 90, and 92. A similar type of oversight – both the raising of the note and its subsequent cancellation – was commit-ted by Chopin in *Etude in F minor* op. 25 no. 2, bar 56. In **FE**H ✕ was added before the fourth third, probably by Chopin himself or due to his suggestion. Taking into consideration the above ar-guments, we introduce this correction into the main text.

Bar 44 We give the note b^1 on the last quaver according to **FE** (→**EE**). This note is missing in **GE**. Traces visible in **GE** indicate that it was removed in the course of printing, although it is pos-sible that we are dealing with some sort of incomplete graphic change (e. g. a transference of this note onto a lower staff). At any rate, due to the fact that the authenticity of the changes made in **GE** remains generally unconfirmed, we do not give this version.
L.H. On the last quaver **FE** has mistakenly placed ♯ before $c\#^1$ instead of $e\#^1$.

Bar 45 R.H. The triplets on the sixth and seventh quaver of the bar in **FE** begin with the seventh $d\#^2$-c^3. In **FE**D and **FE**S Chopin corrected these obvious mistakes. **GE** and **EE** contain the proper version.

p. 46

Bar 51 L.H. In some of the later collected editions the third qua-ver was arbitrarily changed from $f\#^1$ to $d\#^1$.

The reduction of the orchestra part

Bar 52 **FE**^{piano} (→**EE**) and **MFr** did not record the moment of the return to the tempo after *rallentando* in bar 51. Nonetheless, the directive *a tempo* is found in the strings parts in **FE**^{orch} (→**GE**).

Bar 53 We give the dotted rhythm in the lower voices on the fourth beat according to **FE**^{piano} (→**GE**^{piano},**EE**). **MFr**^{orch} and **FE**^{orch} (→**GE**^{orch}) contain (Vno II and Vc.) equal quavers. Cf. comment-ary to bar 1.

The solo part

Bar 56 R.H. **FE** (→**GE**1,**EE**) have no tie sustaining $g\#^2$. This error was corrected in **FE**S.

Bar 57 and 60 R.H. In **FE**H the arpeggio was added before first chord in both bars. Cf. bars 16 and 19.

Bars 58-61 R.H. In this fragment Chopin saw an opportunity for a variant development of the basic version, as evidenced by annotations added in all the extant pupil's copies. We give them arranged according to the degree of certitude with which they can be deciphered and placed.

Variant no. 1 comes from **FE**H. The character of the script does not exclude Chopin's handwriting, but the authenticity of the variant is confirmed primarily by stylistic features:

– a prolongation of the scale by an octave (bars 58-59) is encountered upon many occasions in the annotations made by Chopin in pupil's copies, e. g. in *Etude in F minor* op. 25 no. 2, bar 67 or *Waltz in A♭* op. 34 no. 1, bars 163-164 and 167-168;

– the repetition of one note (four $c\#^3$ in bar 59) is one of Chopin's favourite melodic devices, cf., e. g. bar 29 in this movement of the *Concerto* and *Concerto in F minor* op. 21, II mov., bar 76, *Allegro de Concert* op. 46, bar 87, *Nocturne in B♭ minor* op. 9 no. 1, bar 1, *in E♭* op. 9 no. 2, bar 18, *in G minor* op. 37 no. 1, bar 16; the concurrence of this part of the variant with variant 2, undoubtedly written by Chopin and originating from another copy, is significant.

Variant no. 2. was sketched – probably by Chopin – in **FE**D.

We situate the repeated notes $c\#^3$ in both variants in a place corresponding to their record – before a^1 in the L.H. in **FE**H and before $c\#^3$ on the fourth beat in **FE**D. It is not certain, however, whether this corresponds closely to the execution foreseen by Chopin (cf. *Performance Commentary*).

Variant no. 3 was added in **FE**S carefully, but in someone else's handwriting. Nevertheless, its authenticity is guaranteed by the cult with which J. Stirling, the owner of the copy, surrounded Chopin's person and work, and the devotion with which she gathered the composer's directives in her collection of first editions. Basic doubts may be produced by the location of the variant :

– this arpeggio, encompassing five quavers, is recorded on the margin of the page, next to bars 59-62; it could be sensibly situated both above the sextuplet in bar 59 (as the arpeggio in A major) and after the chord in bar 61 (as the arpeggio in A minor); the record of the variant without key signature or any accidentals permits both those possibilities;

– in the light of classical norms, the process of halting the developing musical narrative in its climax on the paused minim $c\#^3$ in bar 59 creates a natural opportunity for the introduction of this type of figure; this is the version we give above the main text;

– the texturally affiliated figuration, added in this passage in **FE**H, and the perfect concurrence (as regards the used notes and even the position of the hand) of the beginning of the arpeggio and the preceding chord, as well as the end and the following chord in bar 62, speak in favour of situating the arpeggio in bar 61; we take this possibility into consideration in a footnote.

Bar 59 R.H. **FE** (→**EE**) has a slur between the notes $c\#^3$. Considering the multiple repetition of $c\#^3$ in Chopin's variants added in this bar in **FE**D and **FE**H, it seems improbable that Chopin did not wish at all to repeat this note in the basic version. Probably, therefore, this sign does not indicate the tying of $c\#^3$, but is only supposed to emphasise the necessity of sustaining the minim. We encounter this type of tenuto-slurs in several compositions by Chopin, e. g. *Ballade in G minor* op. 23, bars 87-88, *Etude in A minor* op. 25 no. 4, bar 30. In this particular case, we do not give it in order to avoid vagueness (cf. commentary to *Waltz in E♭*, op. 18, bar 12, 36, 44).

The reduction of the orchestra part

Bar 63 L.H. The variant comes from **FE**H. The harmonic transition in bars 63-64, performed on one piano, sounds smoother in this version.

The solo part

Bars 64-65 L.H. Some of the later collected editions arbitrarily added lower sixths on the fourth quavers – $f\#$ in bar 64 and $g\#$ in bar 65.

Bar 72 R.H. There is no ♯ above ᴧᴧ in sources. Chopin was very imprecise in the notation of accidentals next to ornaments.

Bar 73 L.H. **FE** has mistakenly $f\#$ on the second quaver. In **FE**S Chopin corrected it to $d\#$ (this version was introduced also in **GE**). In **FE**H ✗ was added prior to the mistaken note, which is a "routine" supplementation, made probably by a pupil, without taking into consideration the structure of the accompaniment in bars 71-76. An identical change was made also in **EE**.
R.H. In **FE** (→**EE**,**GE**1→**GE**2) there is no tie between the grace-note and the minim $d\#^2$.

Bar 77 L.H. In **FE**^{piano} there is only one ♯ before the seventh quaver, at the level of b, so that it is unclear whether it pertains to the lower note of the third (giving $a\#$) or to the upper one (giving $c\#^1$). In the orchestral chord $c\#^1$ is to be found (Vla) in both **MF**r^{orch} and **FE**^{orch}. There emerge two possibilities:

1. **FE**^{piano} does not contain a distinct error, but ♯, raising a to $a\#$ (necessary), was merely placed somewhat too high; this leads to the version with $c\#\#^1$ (the ✗ from the first half of the bar is binding), in which $c\#^1$ of the violas is a passing note.
While reading **FE**^{piano} this version appears to be natural, and this is precisely how the passage was interpreted in **GE** (adding, however, ✗ in the part of the violas) and **EE**. Possibly, this is also the way it was played during lessons by Chopin's pupils; hence the absence of corrections in pupils' copies might indicate $c\#\#^1$;

2. In **FE**^{piano} Chopin intended ♯ to restore $c\#^1$, while the sharpening of a, obvious in the face of sharps in the R.H., was overlooked.
The undoubted $c\#^1$ in the part of the violas speaks decidedly in favour of this version, because a chord note is more likely to be used in this kind of orchestral accompaniment.
This possibility also seems indicated by the pedalling, since the release (or change) of the pedal prior to the fourth beat would not be necessary in the version with $c\#\#^1$ (cf. authentic pedalling in a similar harmonic context in *Fantaisie in F minor* op. 49, bar 18).

The reduction of the orchestra part

p. 48   *Bar 87* R.H. In **FE**^{piano} (→**GE**^{piano},**EE**) the minim $c\#^2$ is placed mistakenly on the second beat.

The solo part

Bar 88 and 90 R.H. **FE** (→**GE**,**EE**) has no ♯ restoring $c\#^2$ in the last third of the third beat. Moreover, **FE** does not have ♯ raising a^2 to $a\#^2$ on the fourth beat.

Bar 91 R.H. In this bar, Chopin's fingering comes from **FE**S, in which the number 3 is additionally written above the tenth semiquaver; this is probably a mistake. See: commentary to bar 116.
R.H. In **FE** the rhythmic division of the fourth beat is uncertain – the figure 5 is placed above the fourth semiquaver out of a group of five. Either the correct number was written imprecisely ('5' describing the quintuplet should be situated above the third note) or the engraver mistakenly wrote '5' instead of the '3' which defines the three last semiquavers as a triplet. None of the pupil's copies contains directives concerning the rhythm. For the purposes of the main text we accept the first possibility, based on the premise that the **FE** notation albeit imprecise, is not mistaken. The version with the quintuplet, recorded precisely, is found in **GE** and **EE**.
The third penultimate semiquaver in **FE** (→**EE**) has mistakenly the value of a crotchet – cf. analogous bar 42. **GE** omitted the prolongation of this note.
The *ossia* variant was added – most probably by Chopin – in **FE**H. A similar pianistic device was applied by the composer in *Nocturne in D♭* op. 27 no. 2, bar 38 (main text and variant).

p. 49   *Bar 94* R.H. The note $e\#^4$ on the second quaver of the bar in **FE** has the value of a semiquaver. The successive group of twenty notes, however, coincides precisely with the third and fourth L.H. quaver. This manner of alignment of the quavers of the accompaniment certainly corresponds to notation in [**A**] and proves that Chopin intended $e\#^4$ to be a quaver. We give this version as the only one; it is also to be found in **EE**. In **GE** the rhythm is totally mistaken – both tied *e#⁴* are semiquavers, and the third and fourth L.H. quaver was arbitrarily shifted below *a#³* and *g#²* (**GE**1→**GE**2) or *f##³* and *f##²* (**GE**3).

R.H. The rhythmic division of the fourth beat, given by us, is contained in **FE** (→**EE**). In **GE**1 (→**GE**2), the whole group of 6 notes was mistakenly linked by a demisemiquaver beam. In **GE**3 this mistake was erroneously revised by adding the number 6 and shifting the last quaver in the L.H. below *f##²*. This completely arbitrary version was accepted in the majority of the later collected editions, as a rule changing the beam to a semiquaver one in order to achieve rhythmic correctness.

Bar 103 R.H. The second grace-note in the third figure in **GE** is mistakenly *b²* instead of *g#²*. This error was probably found also in **FE**, where, however, it was corrected in the last phase of proofreading.

Both parts

p. 50 *Bars 104-105* In **MFr**ʷ the marking *a tempo* is in bar 104, and in **FE**ᵖⁱᵃⁿᵒ (→**EE**) – in bar 105. **GE** has arbitrarily *Tempo 1°* in bar 104.

The solo part

Bar 108 L.H. In **FE** (→**GE**) the second note is *d#*. In **FE**D and **FE**S Chopin corrected this obvious mistake.

L.H. The numeral of fingering (1) is added below the seventh semiquaver in **FE**S in the handwriting of the pupil. This is certainly a mistake – such fingering would be contrary to numerals written undoubtedly by Chopin in bar 106. See: commentary to bar 116.

Bar 112 R.H. The sixth note in **FE** (→**EE**,**GE**1→**GE**2) is *a²*. Chopin corrected this mistake in **FE**S.

Bar 113 L.H. The sixth note in **FE** (→**GE**,**EE**) is *f#²*, which in **FE**S Chopin changed to *e²*. In the original version the transition from *f#²* to *e²* between the sixth and eighth semiquaver corresponded to the transition *f#¹-e¹* in the part of the violas (the first and second beat). In the **FE**S version the piano part is treated more independently – the same note (*e²*) appears on the sixth, eight and tenth semiquaver three times, as in analogous figures in the previous two bars. The figurate background of the theme thus becomes smoother and more uniform as regards sonority, which in this context should be recognised as improvement. We cannot totally exclude the possibility that this change is a correction of a note imprecisely written in [**A**]. This is the reason why we accept *e²* as the only text.

Some of the later collected editions left the original *f#²* on the sixth semiquaver, and arbitrarily changed *e²* to *f#²* on the eighth and tenth semiquaver.

p. 51 *Bar 116* R.H. The second half of the bar in **FE**S contains the numerals 1 written in pencil by Chopin above the third semiquaver in each triplet. J. Stirling inked in the majority of Chopin's pencilled fingering in this movement of the *Concerto*; in doing so, she did not avoid several errors (cf. commentaries to bar 91 and 108). In the discussed passage she mistakenly wrote only a single 1 above the first *e²* in the seventh triplet.

III. Rondo. Vivace

The reduction of the orchestra part

p. 52 *Bar 1 and 5* L.H. The third quaver in **FE**ᵖⁱᵃⁿᵒ (→**GE**ᵖⁱᵃⁿᵒ) is *B₁-G#* in bar 1 and *A₁-G#* in bar 5. The *G#₁-G#* octave which occurs in both **MFr**ᵒʳᶜʰ and **FE**ᵒʳᶜʰ (→**GE**ᵒʳᶜʰ) proves that these are errors.

The solo part

Bar 20 The simultaneous sounding of the second grace-note with the L.H. chord was marked by Chopin in **FE**D.

p. 54 *Bar 61* R.H. The main text comes from **FE** (→**EE**,**GE**1→**GE**2). We may doubt whether the almost unnoticeable rhythmic variant occurring here (in relation to analogous bars 60, 288 and 289) was intended by Chopin. Similar types of imprecise notation took place in Chopin's works, cf., e. g. commentary to bar 377. This is the reason why we give as a variant the version concurrent with the remaining bars (it appears also in **GE**3).

Bar 62 and 290 L.H. **GE** does not have note *d#²* on the fourth beat in bar 62. The oversight on the part of the engraver of **GE** is evidenced by a comparison with analogous bar 290, in which all the sources have the third *b¹-d#²*. In some of the later collected editions the mistaken version of bar 62 was applied also in bar 290.

Bars 66-67 and 294-295 L.H. In **FE** the notes *e¹* in the second half of bar 66 and 294 have the value of quavers. Nonetheless, the note in bar 294 is tied with *e¹* in the following bar; consequently, we add to it the necessary prolongation dot. In order not to render both passages complicated due to a differentiation, which in praxis is unheard, we suggest that *e¹* be tied also in bars 66-67.

In **GE** the tie sustaining *e¹* is absent in both those passages. This fact could indicate that Chopin did not add it until the last stage of proof-reading **FE**.

Bar 67 L.H. The note *a* in the first quaver in **FE** (→**GE**,**EE**) has mistakenly the value of a crotchet. Cf. bar 295.

p. 55 *Bar 93* R.H. The majority of the later collected editions arbitrarily added ∿ above *f#²*.

The reduction of the orchestra part

p. 56 *Bars 126-127* The following erroneous version appears in later copies of **GE**2: 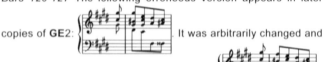. It was arbitrarily changed and supplemented in **GE**3 on the basis of **GE**ᵒʳᶜʰ:

The solo part

Bar 139 L.H. In **FE** (→**EE**) and **MFr**ᵒʳᶜʰ *g#* occurs as the first note in the bass, while in **FE**ᵒʳᶜʰ the cello part has even a precautionary # before this note (after *g* occurring four bars earlier). In the pupils' copies Chopin also did not introduce any changes. **GE** arbitrarily added ♮ before the discussed note, thus lowering *g#* to *g*. This unauthentic version was included in the decisive majority of the later collected editions.

p. 58 *Bars 167-168* L.H. **GE** does not have a tie sustaining *e*.

The reduction of the orchestra part

Bar 177 Before the third quaver **FE**ᵖⁱᵃⁿᵒ (→**GE**ᵖⁱᵃⁿᵒ,**EE**) has no ♮ lowering *d#¹* to *d¹*. Natural is in the second violins part in **FE**ᵒʳᶜʰ (→**GE**ᵒʳᶜʰ) and in **MFr**ᵒʳᶜʰ.

Bar 187 R.H. **FE**piano (→**GE**ᵖⁱᵃⁿᵒ,**EE**) has, obviously mistakenly, only *f* as the first quaver (in **FE** and **EE** without ♮). We give the F-major chord, similarly to all analogous passages and in accordance with **FE**ᵒʳᶜʰ (→**GE**ᵒʳᶜʰ) and **MFr**ᵒʳᶜʰ.

The solo part

Bar 196 Here, **FE** contains a rhythmic error in both hands: ♪ ♩ . It is necessary either to add the overlooked prolongation dots next to the second notes, or to remove the superfluous quaver flags next to the first notes. The first of those corrections was introduced in **EE**, and the second – in **GE**. The latter possibility (our main text) appears to be more probable for moderating the course of the music (*rallentando* in the next bar). In an analogous context equal crotchets appear in bar 440. Nonetheless, the absence of corrections in pupils' copies speaks in favour of a rhythm with a quaver at the beginning of the bar (our variant).

Bar 203 R.H. The grace-notes in **FE** erroneously sound *c#³-d#³*.

p. 60

Bar 225 R.H. The sixth semiquaver in **FE** is *a³*. This indubitable mistake is evidenced by the following arguments:
– bars 224-225 are a sequential repetition of bars 220-221, and the discussed note is the last in the nine-semiquaver figure which comprises a central motif of the figuration in those bars:

 ; this figure is repeated three more times in bars 228-230; both upon the first occasion (bar 221) and in further repetitions (bars 228-230) the last two semiquavers of this figure form an octave interval;
– a repetition of *a³* at the top of the passage in this bar would disturb the regularity of motion also as regards execution, thus constituting an unjustified complication.
In this passage in **FE**H we find a correction, which, however, pertains to the seventh semiquaver (a change of *a³* to *b³*). In the light of the above cited argumentation this change should be regarded as mistaken.
L.H. In some of the later collected editions *d#¹* was arbitrarily changed to *f#¹* in the chord on the second beat.

Bar 228 R.H. Some of the later collected editions arbitrarily added to the *g#¹-g#²* octave the note *b¹*, tied to *b¹* in the previous bar (analogously to bars 223-224). With all certainty Chopin intentionally did not sustain this note, since in bar 227, due to the *legato* in the upper voice, it is much more comfortable to play the second *a¹-b¹* with the first finger also on the fourth quaver, which makes it impossible to sustain *b¹*. (A different arrangement of the black keys in the upper voice melody is the reason why this difficulty does not appear in bars 223-224).

Bar 230 R.H. The last semiquaver in **FE** (→**GE**1→**GE**2) is mistakenly *a³*. See: commentary to bar 225.
L.H. At the beginning of the bar **GE** has erroneously only *e#¹*.

Bar 233 and 235 R.H. **FE** (→**EE**,**GE**1→**GE**2) has *c#³* on the second quaver of those bars. Chopin did not introduce any changes also in the pupils' copies. In **GE**3 naturals lowering *c#³* to *c³* were arbitrarily added before the discussed notes. Presumably, the reviser regarded such close proximity between *c#³* and *c²* in the last triplet of the lower voice to be improbable. Nonetheless, this type of a close juxtaposition occurs in several of Chopin's works, e. g. in *Etude in E* op. 10 no. 3, bars 54-55. In an already obvious situation in analogous bar 239, the absence of the indispensable ♮ lowering *d#³* to *d³* in **GE**1 (→**GE**2; as well as in **FE**) additionally confirmed the conviction of the reviser of **GE**3 about the necessity of adding ♮ prior to *c#³*.
The unauthentic version with *c³* was included in the decisive majority of the later collected editions.

Bar 237 L.H. The fourth *b-e#¹* on the second quaver occurs in all the sources. The majority of the later collected editions arbitrarily added to it *c#¹*. The absence of *c#¹* could by justified by the logic of linking the chords in bars 236-237: *b-e¹* in chords in bar 236 changes to *b-e#¹* in bar 237.

Bars 250-251 L.H. In **GE** and the majority of the later collected editions the second and fourth figure were exchanged so that at the end of bar 250 there is a semiquaver triplet, and at the end of bar 251 – two semiquavers. Originally, this mistake also occurred in **FE**, where, however, Chopin corrected it in the last stage of the proofs. The **FE** version is confirmed by the fingering added by Chopin in **FE**D.

Bar 254 and 258 The marking ***p*** in bar 254 occurs in **FE** (→**EE**). It is absent in **GE**, and some of the later collected editions based on it arbitrarily added ***f*** in both bars.

Bars 256-257 The *8ᵛᵃ* sign above the second R.H. figure (starting with the fourth quaver in bar 256) was added in **FE**H, possibly by Chopin. It seems much more probable that its author intended it to pertain to both hands' parts, which we take into consideration in the *ossia* variant.

p. 62

Bar 263 and 267 R.H. In the second half of both those bars in **FE** there is no ♮ lowering *g#¹* to *g¹*. This is most probably a mistake made by Chopin – *g¹* in bar 263 stems naturally from the preceding G-major scale (here **EE** and **GE** added ♮), and it is confirmed by *g¹* in a similar passage in bar 265. This whole section (bars 263-267) in **GE** lacks several other indispensable accidentals, which proves that in this respect Chopin did not check this fragment very carefully.

Bar 279 R.H. In some of the later collected editions the second quaver of the triplet was arbitrarily changed from *d#²* to *b¹*.

p. 63

Bar 280 and 281 L.H. In both bars in **FE** (→**GE**1→**GE**2) the third quaver is the sixth *g#-e¹*. **EE** has this sixth only in bar 281, and in bar 280 it contains, probably mistakenly, the chord *e-g#-e¹*. In **GE**3 this chord was arbitrarily introduced in both bars. We give the sixths occurring in **FE** as undoubtedly intended by Chopin, who in this way referred to the outline of the accompaniment delineated in the preceding eight bars.

Bar 283 L.H. We give the accompaniment found in **FE** (→**EE**, **GE**1→**GE**2). In **GE**3 and the majority of the later collected editions the lower note of the second quaver was arbitrarily changed from *f#* to *a*. Some of the remaining later collected editions arbitrarily changed the lower note of the fourth eighth from *a* to *f#*.

Bars 288-289 R.H. In some of the later collected editions the last two notes in each of these bars were arbitrarily given the value of semiquavers (analogously to bars 60-61). A different slurring of these pairs of bars entitles us to presuppose that also the rhythmic differences are not accidental. Chopin probably treated these passages independently, and subtly differentiated them – cf. *Performance Commentary* to bars 60-63 and 288-291.

p. 65

Bar 358 R.H. In **FE** (→**EE**,**GE**1→**GE**2) the use of the first finger is marked above the fourth semiquaver. This indubitable mistake was corrected by Chopin in **FE**D.

p. 66

Bars 373-374 R.H. In **FE** (→**EE**) there is no tie sustaining *d²* over the bar line. This is probably an oversight, since in an analogous passage in bars 377-378 *g¹* is sustained. **GE** has ties in both places.

p. 67

Bar 377 L.H. On the second quaver of the bar **FE** (→**GE**,**EE**) has two equal semiquavers. This is probably an error, since no arguments speak in favour of differentiating this bar in relation to analogous bar 373 (we cannot exclude the possibility that a similar mistake occurred in bar 61 – cf. commentary). Dotted rhythm in the orchestra part occurs in the first violins in **FE**ᵒʳᶜʰ (→**GE**ᵒʳᶜʰ) and in the cellos in **GE**ᵒʳᶜʰ; it is also contained – in both parts – in **MF**rᵒʳᶜʰ. In this situation, equal semiquavers in the cello part in **FE**ᵒʳᶜʰ should be recognized as a repetition of the erroneous script of the piano part. It should be added that when such rhythms appear against the triplets background, both their forms could, in Chopin's script, denote the same execution – the second of the semiquavers or a demisemiquaver simultaneously with the third note in the triplet, see: e. g. *Ballade in F minor* op. 52, bars 217-220, 223 and 225.

Bars 384-385 R.H. In **FE** (→**GE**1→**GE**2) the octave *e²-e³* is not tied. The ties were supplemented in **EE** and **GE**3, which seems to be justified by the presence of ties in similar L.H. motifs in bars 380-381 and 382-383.

Bar 385 R.H. The octave b^2-b^3 at the end of the bar, notated together with the first two quavers of the following bar by using an 8va sign, occurs in **FE** ($\rightarrow$**EE**,**GE**1$\rightarrow$**GE**2). In **GE**3 it was replaced by the octave b^1-b^2, possibly due to an error made while changing the notation into a version without the transposition sign. This unauthentic version was accepted in the decisive majority of the later collected editions. The original version is more comfortable from the viewpoint of execution.

Bars 392-394, 396-398 and 400-401 L.H. In the second half of bar 393 **FE** has a slur (tie?) running from $d\#^1$ or $f\#^1$, but lacks its end in bar 394 (on the next page). In this manner, the meaning of the sign is unclear: it could be a slur $d\#^1$-e^1 or a tie to $f\#^1$. **GE**1 ($\rightarrow$**GE**2) accepted the first possibility, and **EE** – both possibilities (slurs and ties both in this passage and in bars 397-398). We also cannot exclude the possibility that the tie was placed in this bar by mistake, e. g. instead of the tie sustaining $f\#^1$ in bars 392-393 (cf. the sign in bars 400-401). Taking into consideration the above doubts, and in order not to complicate the text by unessential variants based on surmises, we do not give this sign (this is the version in **GE**3).
In some of the later collected editions ties sustaining $f\#^1$ in those bars were rendered uniform, from the addition of ties in all five passages to their total removal.

p. 69 *Bars 442-443* L.H. Some of the later collected editions mistakenly included into the solo part the tied quaver *B* at the beginning of bar 443. In all the sources this note is printed small, since it belongs only to the orchestra part.

Bar 450 R.H. In **FE** the second quaver (e^3) was printed at the proper height, but without a ledger line going through the note. In **GE** and **EE** this became the reason for its mistaken deciphering as $d\#^3$ (the error in **EE** was subsequently corrected in the course of printing). In **FE**J the missing line was added, probably by Chopin.

p. 71 *Bar 482* R.H. Before the sixth semiquaver **FE** mistakenly has ♯ instead of ♮. This error is corrected in **FE**J.

p. 119 *Bar 488* R.H. The fourth semiquaver in **FE** ($\rightarrow$**EE**,**GE**1$\rightarrow$**GE**2) is $a\#^1$. In **GE**3 and the majority of the later collected editions it was arbitrarily changed to a^1. This type of an anticipation of harmony by means of notes of the figuration is characteristic for Chopin's works, cf., e. g. bar 279 in this movement of the *Concerto* or *Ballade in G minor* op. 23, bar 63. In the harmonically similar bar 492 the preceding figuration creates a different melodic context, so that a^1 occurring there does not constitute an argument in favour of an eventual mistaken placing of ♯ in the discussed bar.

Jan Ekier
Paweł Kamiński